My Dream Flights

My Dream
Flights

Patricia Pearce MBE

My Dream Flights

A catalogue record for this book is available from the British Library.

Design and artwork by Pentacor Media Ltd, High Wycombe, Bucks

Printed by Image Evolution Ltd, Aldermaston, Berkshire

ISBN 978-0-9570163-0-9

First published in the UK in 2012 by Patricia Pearce MBE

Dedication

. . . .

I would like to thank my Mum for being such an inspiration to me my whole life. She made me the person I am.

To thank my brother Derek and sister-in-law Beth and the rest of my family for the support they have given me over the years with Dreamflight.

To all my friends and people whose lives have crossed my path, thank you so much for giving me so much.

Patricia Pearce MBE

Contents

PART 1:
My Flying Years

1. My Childhood Dream to be an Air Hostess

I was just nine years old when I made up my mind that I wanted to be a BOAC stewardess. We lived just a few miles from London Heathrow Airport so I suppose it was inevitable. I would read every book in the library about life as a stewardess. When I reached my teenage years I went to Twickenham Technical School (the commercial section at Hampton Middlesex). There were two boys in my class Melvyn Taylor and Peter Iggulden, who were both as keen on aircraft as I was (to this day, some 40 odd years later, Melvyn and I keep in touch at Christmas times. He and his wife live in New Zealand). At weekends the three of us would go "aircraft spotting" at Heathrow. We would log down all the aircraft registrations. Another favourite pastime was to collect airline timetables. I would write off to every airline whose address I could get hold of and they would sometimes send postcards of the aircraft as well. My mother often complained that I had two suitcases full of this memorabilia. I wish I had kept them as some of them would raise a fair amount of money on eBay now!

I studied shorthand and typing and was trained as a secretary. My first job was in London working for a company called Federated Foundaries just off of Oxford Street. This lasted for just a year, which was a great experience, but, yes you have guessed it, I wanted to work at the airport.

I landed the job as secretary to Geoffrey Corbin who was the Commercial Manager of a small airline called BKS Air Transport. I was told before I went for the interview that he was looking for someone older than me (I was 17 at the time), but the agency felt I had the right skills and told me "just try to make yourself look older"! What would you have done?

Fortunately for me, I was successful and I spent three wonderful years working for Geoff. It was a very good all round training, far more than just shorthand and typing. I had only been working for Geoff for three weeks when he had to go into hospital. What a baptism of fire. As Commercial Manager Geoff was responsible for all the commercial side of the airline. He was responsible for applying to the Air Transport Licensing Board for licences to fly on certain routes. It was like going to court, you had to put up a case and then he would be put in the "witness" box and be cross examined as to why you needed the licence on that route. Other airlines would be there trying to stop you getting the licence. He was also responsible for the charter side of the airline. One part of the charter side was the transport of horses and in particular race horses. Initially we had a Bristol Freighter and then a converted Airspeed Ambassador (Elizabethan). We were responsible for working out the price of the charters, getting the contract signed, and then advising the Operations Department, who would organise a crew for the flight. As the Operations Department and Crew Check-in was in the same building as us, I got to know the various crews. As I was desperate to fly, I would ask the captains if I could go with them on the weekend flights and make their tea. Life in the airline industry was so much easier in those days, we didn't have all the security problems that we have nowadays, and most weekends I would go flying.

Reservations was also in the same building and being a very small company we would take it in turns to be rostered to work in the Reservations department on a Saturday morning. It gave you an all round background of the airline industry and I was in my element. I loved every aspect of it. Many of the friends I made way back between 1962 – 1966 are still my treasured friends today.

Although I was thoroughly enjoying my job, my plan to become a stewardess was still foremost in my mind. BKS ran one training programme a year and this took place in March up in Newcastle. You had to be 21 to apply. I was not 21 until July and didn't want to wait until the next March. How impatient we can be at that age! I found out that Channel Airways, based at Southend-on-Sea, took crew younger than this so I applied to them and was offered the job. I only spent three months working there which was great fun but really hard work. Cabin crews these days do not realise what we had to do in those days. I worked on DC3s, DC4s, Viscount 700s, Bristol Freighters and a Doves. My first flight was on the 8th May 1965 on a Viscount from Southend to Ostend. Oh the glamour! On standby days we had to go and work in the kitchens helping with the salads, etc. All of a sudden you would be called to wash your hands and go off on a flight to somewhere in Europe. Before a flight, you would go round the Catering Unit and collect all your soft drinks, toilet rolls etc., and then beg someone to carry it to your aircraft for you. If not, you carried it yourself. We also did not receive "allowances" like the crews do today, but the Captain had an allowance for our meals. So if you wanted to eat, you had to go out with your flight crew. On a DC3 you were the only stewardess, so I once saw every night club in Ostend trying to get a meal out of my flight crew! The answer when I said I was hungry was the standard answer "just one more drink." If they had just fed me I would have gone back to the hotel and left them to enjoy themselves.

I used to go back to the offices of BKS to see my friends. Being such a small airline they all knew how much I had wanted to fly but hadn't realised that I would leave them and go and work for another airline. I was back visiting one day when the Chief Pilot asked if I would like to return and fly for them and so on the 17th July 1965 I did my first flight on a Viscount from Heathrow to Leeds/Bradford and return. I was now working on Bristol Britannia 102s, Viscounts, Airspeed Ambassadors (Elizabethan) and Avro 748 aircraft. How much I enjoyed being back amongst my friends and not having to work in the kitchens on standby.

For the next year I enjoyed myself flying for BKS, but at the back of my mind was still the romantic idea of flying for BOAC. However, I was trying to gain as much experience as I could. I went to Newcastle, Leeds/ Bradford and Teeside on a regular basis, and overseas to Oporto, San Sebastian, Bilbao and also to Amsterdam, Dublin, Belfast and Jersey. At weekends we used to do holiday charter flights to Palma, Tangier, and

Perpignan. These were a laugh and the things passengers used to bring back from Palma. Great big toys such as donkeys, sombrero hats, etc. I will leave you to cast your minds back to things you used to bring back.

By the summer of 1966 I had decided the time had come to apply to BOAC and see if I could realise my dream of doing long haul flying. I remember one of the questions I was asked at the interview was "Do you think you could cope with romantic stopovers and advances made by some of the flight crew?" My reply "I had had many night stops in Newcastle, etc. and I was sure I would be able to cope."

I applied to BOAC and was accepted and started my flying training in July 1966.

2. My Flying Career
with BOAC/BA

In July 1966 I started my training. It was a six week course and thoroughly enjoyable. We covered subjects such as how to handle passengers, mixing cocktails, how to serve meals and wine, and currency conversions (as we had to collect money for the drinks in those days). We had to learn about the items of duty free goods we would be selling and the prices of these. We spent hours in the "mock-up" practising all these skills.

The deportment and make up sessions were great. The beauticians from Elizabeth Arden gave us make up hints and taught us how to walk down a catwalk. Medical was very interesting, learning CPR and how to recognise symptoms of heart attacks, etc.

The uniform fitting was what we all enjoyed the most and couldn't wait until the day we received our brand new uniforms. We all felt so proud. That first uniform is the one I still think that I felt the smartest in.

Safety and Equipment Procedures (SEP)

We also spent a great deal of time on Safety and Equipment Procedures. We had to be able to use and locate the oxygen, lifejackets, etc. and how to evacuate an aircraft. We had to learn about desert and arctic survival. We were taken to Hounslow swimming baths to inflate the liferafts and learn how to swim around in the water with a lifejacket on and be able to clamber in to one of the rafts (not easy with the lifejacket on believe you me). We had to go into a smoke filled chamber and locate passengers (dummies, I hasten to add) and learn how to operate fire extinguishers and put out oven fires. These procedures would be repeated every year at our annual SEP Check. A date that every crew member dreads and is really glad when it is over. Over the years some of the procedures have also changed. For instance, when defibrillators were put on board every crew member had to know how to use them. With the modern days of technology the exams are done on a computer now.

You had to pass all sections of the course and at the very end there was the "Wings" ceremony. By now we all had our uniforms but the one thing that was missing was the wings that you would have to sew on before you went on your first flight. There was a great deal of excitement on that day. We were instructed on how to sit for the photograph, (all legs had to be facing the same way) and we were so excited as we were going to be told where our first flight was going to be and which fleet we would be allocated to. Either the VC10 or the 707 fleet. I was also extremely surprised as I was awarded the "Golden Ashtray" which was for the best trainee award. I couldn't wait to get home and tell my Dad. He was really so opposed to me flying but I think he then realised how much it all meant to me. I had arrived in BOAC and in style!

I was allocated to the VC10 fleet. I was thrilled as several years earlier I had been to the Vickers factory in Weybridge to see them being built. The father of one of the boys in my youth club worked at the factory so we were very privileged to be allowed so close to them. Now I was going to be working on one. There were two types of VC10, the standard and the larger Super VC10.

My first trip was as a supernumary crew member (that means extra crew), to New York for a nightstop. I had always wanted to go to New York and I was so thrilled. The flight went OK and we boarded the crew bus at the airport to go to Manhattan. Driving in you could see the skyline of the Empire State building and the Statue of Liberty. We went through the tunnel and came up on Manhattan Island. It really is a concrete jungle and my first impressions were of steaming manholes in the roads. I was quite disappointed. After a quick shower it was off to meet the rest of the crew in the hotel lobby and go to the usual "crew bar" which was called McCann's. Something that would be repeated many times on subsequent trips to New York!

The next morning we met up for breakfast just round the corner from the hotel, and then off to do some shopping. Back at lunchtime and a couple of hours sleep (well just resting in my case, as I was so excited about the flight back).

In those days BOAC operated in and out of Terminal 3 at Heathrow. After landing we were allowed to go in to the terminal building and have breakfast as we were given a voucher for this. Not everyone went, but I was still on a high from the flight, so I did.

I couldn't wait to get my next roster. Back then the flight crew names were on the roster as well, this was in days before the flight crew had a bid line system for their trips. My next trip was a Khartoum–Aden– Khartoum trip. We operated down to Khartoum and the experienced crew explained to me that we had to take all the "mixes" (tonic, ginger ale, etc.) off of the aircraft not just for our crew but also for the crew ahead of us. That crew would be getting on and flying a shuttle from Khartoum to Aden and back and they would go to the NAAFI in Aden and buy the spirits for the two crews. We had arrived in the morning so went to bed for the day and the other crew would be back in the evening with the "booze" and we would all meet up. We arranged a day trip out in to the desert in jeeps – obviously something that I had never done before. This was much better than going backwards and forwards to Newcastle or Leeds/Bradford every day.

The crew of a VC10 consisted of ten members. Captain, 2 First Officers, Flight Engineer, Chief Steward, two stewards and 3 stewardesses. We were treated very well in those days.

Every trip was an adventure for me back then in the 1960s. Our trips lasted from 3 days to 21 days. The 21 day ones were "round the world." As the fleets were not as large as they are nowadays, the chances of flying with the same people came up more often than they do now. There were many great characters of Chief Stewards then. Many of them had worked as stewards on the ships and had then turned to aircraft. Many of the Captains had been in the RAF and had flown during the war. I can remember flying with one captain who had been one of the "Dambusters" and he had some really interesting stories to tell us.

I can remember my first trip to Nairobi when we stayed at the Grosvenor Hotel (we used to call it the grotty Grosvenor.) I had my first taste of avocado pears there. The more experienced crew were going on about these as an hors d'oeuvres and I just had to try them. Well, I wondered what all the fuss was about, as I didn't think they were anything special, but I must say now I absolutely love them. Mind you, I said the same thing about caviar!

I also had my first experience of a day trip to a game park outside of Nairobi. This was something special. I also remember the fantastic colours of the bouganvillia flowers, the vivid blue of the jacaranda trees and the agapantha flowers. I found Africa so colourful.

We all used to go the market on the day we were due to fly home and order our fruit, vegetables and flowers. The fruit and vegetables (and yes you have guessed) the avocados, were put in baskets and then sewn up. The flowers were put in boxes for us, and we were also given a couple of pineapples each when we boarded the aircraft from the aircraft catering company. The fantastic Birds of Paradise flowers were a must to take home to give to friends and neighbours.

Other places we would also buy boxes of flowers were Singapore, Bangkok and Kuala Lumpur though the flowers here were orchids.

After three years on VC10s the company decided to merge the fleets. I would now be flying on B707s as well as the VC10. I wasn't sure that I was going to like this as the VC10 fleet was known as the "young fleet." Allegedly the flight crew on the 707 were called old "Atlantic Barons" They turned out to be not too bad and I had some great trips on that fleet and it was also interesting to be going to new places.

I remember one of my first flights on the 707 was to Hong Kong. What an experience flying into the old Hong Kong Airport – Kai Tak. I was on the Flight Deck for the landing. The aircraft flew towards a hill which had a red checker board painted on it and at the last minute the aircraft would bank to the right and line up to the runway. You could almost see in the windows of the blocks of flats! Hong Kong is like a concrete jungle and how all those shop keepers made a living is beyond me. Mind you I did my bit to try to keep them in business over the years. A trip up the "Peak" was a must and to have cocktails at sunset up there is a fantastic sight.

The Middle East

When visiting some of the Middle Eastern countries we had to wear the black abayas. In some hotels we were not allowed to eat with the men on our crew unless we went to the family room. We were not allowed to go out by the swimming pool with them. The hotel had a roster and sometimes it would be men in the morning and women in the afternoon and then vice versa.

Further Training over the Years

Of course over the years there would be plenty more training sessions. Each time you were promoted there would be another course. When I started the girls were not allowed to hold any senior position on the crew. You were contracted for ten years or until age 36 and then you left. This did change with the equality act.

When I was promoted to a Stdss 1 this meant I would be working in first class. Back to the training school to learn different techniques and to learn the different standards of address when addressing royalty and other famous and influential people. Some of the cocktails we had to learn how to mix were Manhattan, Negroni, etc. If only I could remember now what went in them.

I used to love working in first class but you had to do your "years down the back" before you were allowed "through the curtain" to work in first class.

The service in those days was I believe was far superior to what it is today. All the food was served from a trolley. The hors d'oeuvres trolley had a rotary wheel on it and from this we would serve caviar, smoked salmon, and oysters (when departing Australia).

Back then we used to carve a joint in the first class section so those skills had to be learnt. We had to learn how to serve caviar with the egg yolk, egg white and chopped onion, together with a small glass of neat vodka. Those of you who know me well will now realise why I love some of the nicer things in life! Soup was served from a large tureen and there would be a full cheese board and decanters for port.

Today things have changed as generally the businessman/woman wants to get on, have a quick meal, and get as much sleep as he/she can. When departing New York they can have the same aircraft meal in the lounge before boarding so they can just sleep the whole flight and then go to the Arrivals Lounge in Heathrow and have breakfast.

I was later promoted to Chief Stewardess and then Purser whilst I was on the B747.

I was posted back to the VC10/707 fleet as a Purser in charge on the aircraft on 9th April 1978. This was the first time that females had been in charge on an aircraft. On 20th May 1980 I was posted back to the B747.

Finally I was promoted to Cabin Service Director for the rest of my career. My first trip as a CSD, as we were known, was to Miami on the 28th June 1986, twenty years after I had joined the company.

When I first joined, stewardesses were given a ten year contract. The age to join was between 21 and 26, so eventually our retirement contract was changed to ten years or age 36. Finally equality came in and the girls were allowed to stay on to the same retirement age as the men.

On the next page I have printed a copy of my first pay slip.

GROSS PAY TO DATE	TAX TO DATE	AIRWAYS PENSION TO DATE	G.P.S. TO DATE	TAX CODE BASIS & WK./MTH.	FIXED PAY OR WAGES
251 7 2	25 4	2 6 0		206 N 5	45 16 8

VARIABLE OR HOLIDAY PAY	ARREARS/ADJ'T OR SICK PAY	GROSS PAY THIS WEEK/MONTH	COIN B/F	STAFF No.	NAME	PAY POINT
	10 7 0	56 3 8		83919	PEARCE PM	12

NON TAXABLE PAYMENTS	COIN C/F	TOTAL THIS WEEK/MONTH	TOTAL DEDUCT'S THIS WEEK/MONTH	NET PAY	M O P	MONTH OR WEEK ENDING
		56 3 8	12 11 6	43 12 2		AUG 66

DEDUCTIONS THIS WEEK/MONTH

A	6 8 0	B	3 17 6	C	2 6 0						

B.O.A.C.
PAY ADVICE
(MONTHLY PAID STAFF - NET PAY
HAS BEEN CREDITED TO YOUR
BANK ACCOUNT.)

KEY TO DEDUCTION CODES

A. Income Tax
B. N. I. Contributions
C. Airways Pension
D. State Grad. Pen.
E. U. K. F. S.
F. Speedbird Club
G. Staff A/C General

H. Staff A/C Loan
I. Staff A/C loss of Lic.
J. H. S. A.
K. Aero Club
L. Hostel
M. Attachment Order
N. Rent

O. Aircrew Sports Com.
P. Savings—Trustee
Q. Savings—Treforest
R. Q. E. A. Pension
S. Other

TAX BASIS CODES

N. Normal
O. Code O
W. Week I
E. Emergency
S. Standard Rate
X. No Tax Liability
A. Amended Tax Free Pay

M. O. P. (Method of Payment)—"C" = Cheque.   Coin C/P will be the amount B/F next week

above: MY FIRST PAY SLIP – and I thought I was rich
being paid £42.12.2d for the MONTH

right: Serving the soup
from a tureen in the first
class cabin of a B747

19

3. Aircraft Types

The types of aircraft that I have flown on are:

1965/66
DC3 – Dakota
DC4
Bristol freighter
Viscount 700
Viscount 800
Dove
Airspeed Ambassador (Elizabethan)
Avro 748
Bristol Britannia (known as the Whispering Giant)

1966 until 2004
Standard VC10
Super VC10
Boeing 707
Boeing 747–200 series (first flight – 3rd May 1975)
Boeing 747–400 series
Boeing 777

A total of 15 types of aircraft.

left: A Dakota of BKS which was the first aircraft that I worked on as cabin crew. This carried 36 passengers

right: The Airspeed Ambassador which held 55 passengers

left: The VC10 (Standard and Super) which was one of my favourites. Affectionately known as the "Iron Duck"

right: The Boeing 707

left: The B747

right: The B777

4. Uniforms

My first uniform was dark green when I worked for Channel Airways based at Southend-on-Sea for just three months.

My second uniform when I worked for BKS Air Transport was navy blue.

above: Taken on board BKS Elizabethan aircraft

My third uniform was my BOAC one. It was my favourite of all times. In total I wore 8 different styles of uniform

At one stage we used to wear a paper dress out of New York and down to the Caribbean. We would travel from the hotel to the airport in

our "normal" uniform and we were given these paper dresses to put on in one of the offices. It had a floral pattern, and we wore flowers in our hair and green plastic shoes with jewels on. We would cut the uniforms to the length we wanted. On my second trip I knew exactly where on the pattern I needed to cut my dress, so I got on the floor and started cutting. The other two stewardesses on my crew said, "while you're down there Pat, you might as well cut ours." This I did, but I forgot that the other girls where quite a bit taller than me! The first pair of tights were given to me by the company as before that time we had only ever worn stockings. The crutch kept slipping down to our knees and we were forever pulling them up.

I remember arriving late at night in the hotel in Kingston, Jamaica, and I think everyone thought we were part of the cabaret.

On other routes we would have one or more national stewardesses on the crew and they would wear their national costumes. On the Japanese route the girls would take quite a while to put on their kimonos. On the Indian and Pakistan flights the girls would wear saris and the Hong Kong route the Hong Kong based girls would wear their

right: Very glamorous
don't you think?

above: Other uniforms I wore during my time with BOAC/British Airways. We used to have summer and winter uniforms

national cheongsam. We also had Jamaican girls on our Caribbean routes.

On routes to some of the places in the middle east our uniform skirts were too short, so they would bring to the aircraft door a floor length material wrap to put on to cover up our legs. Other places we had to wear a headscarf.

I did wear more uniforms over the years but sadly I never kept photos of them.

5. The Trips Themselves

When I first started flying the aircraft were not capable of the long ranges that they achieve today. There was no requirement to have crew rest areas, which is mandatory these days, hence the trips were much shorter.

The 707 fleet used to do a "Round the World flight" and it was 21 days. I really enjoyed those. This was the schedule – London/Zurich/Rome/New Delhi/Bangkok/Hong Kong/Tokyo/Honolulu/San Fransisco and then turn round and do it all the way back again. Through the Pacific was great but I did lose my birthday one year by crossing the date line.

Another favourite trip back in the sixties and seventies was on the VC10 and was called a "Sydney through the West". This trip was certainly a prized trip. You would start off with a nightstop in New York, 2 nights in Los Angles, 2 nights in Honolulu, 2 nights in Fiji, and then two nights in Sydney or Melbourne, and then turn round and do the trip in reverse. What wonderful times we had on those trips

I always remember my first arrival in Honolulu. I was so excited and then disappointed, because when we arrived in the lobby of the hotel at 9 p.m. all I could see were these rather large American ladies in colourful long dresses (called Moo-Moo dresses) and their husbands in matching shirts, but to spoil the whole effect they had rollers in their hair. What a let down. I have to admit that I haven't been there for years, but I would like to go back some time.

I can remember on one trip in Honolulu there was a self service laundry down near the bar on the beach level of the hotel. I was a new crew member and they told me that I had to wash all the shirts for the men on the crew and iron them. There I was in the laundry doing all the ironing and the rest of the crew were in the bar. Occasionally one or other of them would pop in to see if I was doing alright. I complained that I could do with a glass of wine for company whilst doing the ironing. They complied with my request and after several more glasses you can imagine what my ironing was like. Never again did I fall for this trick.

Nowadays with the aircraft able to stay in the air much longer these types of trips no longer exist. A typical trip now is London Singapore or Bangkok, two nights, Sydney one night, back to Singapore or Bangkok for two nights and then home. Just a nine day trip. Bearing in mind that you don't take off till late in the evening of the first day and are back around 5 a.m. on the last day it is almost a seven day trip.

We also used to have to do standby duties. At the time I was flying you would either do one and a half hour standby, four hour standby or twelve hour standby. One and a half hour standby meant you had to be able to get to the airport in an hour and a half. I used to have two suitcases laid out on the spare bed in my house, one small and one large. I would then have a pile of clothes consisting of essentials, ie. underwear, toilet bag, hair assesories, etc., which would go on any trip. When you got the call out it was a mad dash to throw in all you needed grabbing other clothing from the wardrobes. Remember you could be away for two days or twenty one days, and you might be going to hot climates or in the winter to Canada and Northern USA where it was very cold.

In the early days of my flying with BOAC we used to do a ten day standby block in New York. The schedule could take you to the Carribean, to Lima in Peru or back across the Atlantic to Prestwick and Manchester. It was quite good fun, but at the end of ten days you were ready to go home. In those days there were no such things as mobile phones so you couldn't go out during the hours you were on standby.

Jokes Played on New Crew Members
There was a trapdoor in the galley of both the 707 and the VC10 which was called the Lower 41. I cannot remember why it was called that. It had banks of electrical equipment and circuit breakers, etc., and the

new crew member was told that the very last rivet that was put in on an aircraft was always a golden one and called the "Golden Rivet" The poor unsuspecting girl would be taken down there by the Flight Engineer, need I say any more!

On one occasion when I was in charge of a VC10 aircraft the engineer had gone to the lower 41 bay and a new stewardess came up from the back of the aircraft and I said I would explain about an aircraft load sheet to her. I informed her that we had a coffin down in the hold (we hadn't, but she didn't know that), then there was a knock on the galley floor. I jumped off of the hatch and the engineers' hand came up covered in tomato ketchup. She disappeared off to the back of the aicraft so fast.

Another joke would be to rush a new crew member, who was crossing the Equator for the first time, to the flight deck to "see" the equator. Almost always, they fell for it. Did they expect to see a black line?

Also back in the days of the 707 and VC10s the Navigator would have to put the sextant out of the flight deck roof to get the star shots. The navigator would always be willing to show new crew members and they would stand up and put their eyes up close to the sextant which the navigator had covered in black shoe polish. As the crew member left the flight deck to return to the back of the aircraft, they looked like they had two big black panda eyes.

Another favourite trick to play on new crew members was during the life jacket demonstration. This was in the days when the crew had to stand at the front of the cabin and physically don a life jacket to demonstrate to the passengers. The crew would have exchanged the whistle for a tampax, and when the new crew member heard the instruction "and here is a whistle for attracting attention" a few blushes were experienced when a tampax was pulled out of the pocket instead of the whistle.

A joke to see if the passengers were paying attention would be to put some dry ice into a teapot with just a little water and the effect is brilliant. You then walk through the cabin with this teapot bubbling away.

Typical Day of a Crew Member

I know that many of you are keen to know what happens behind the scenes. This explains a typical type of day for a crew member, but remember this is in the days just before I retired in 2004.

After checking in the crew would go to a briefing room where they would all meet up and be "briefed" by the Cabin Service Director. Crews would "bid" for what position they wanted to work in on the aircraft and this was done by seniority. The CSD would give details of the passenger load and any special requirements, i.e. dietary, wheelchair passengers, children, etc. Emergency procedure questions would be asked.

After the briefing the crew would be taken by a crew bus to the aircraft (nowadays I understand they walk through Terminal 5). We only had 7 minutes on the aircraft to prepare it before the ground staff would be wanting the crew to let the passengers board. On a typical long range flight the whole crew would work for approximately the first three to three and a half hours of the flight. The crew would then be split in half, the first half would go "upstairs" to the crew bunk area and have their legal rest of three hours horizontal rest (approximately, depending on the flight time). They would come back and the other half of the crew would have their rest. For the last two hours of the flight the whole crew would be working again as there would be the final meal to be served. Now you know why some of the crew "disappear" during the flight. As I say it is a legal requirement on a long range flight that the crew have what is called "horizontal rest."

The age of technology in the cabin has certainly changed over the years. I remember about three months after 9/11 had happened we were on our way to New York and we were advised that New York Airport had closed again. We were going to have to divert to Philadelphia. We now had the facility of having phones on board for the passengers. Well, after we had advised the passengers of our intended diversion, a number of our businessmen phoned their drivers in New York and got them to set off to Philadelphia to collect them.

We were on our descent in to Philadelphia when we were advised that New York had re-opened, so we did a climb and went on our way back to New York. Can you imagine, all those drivers were now on their way to Philadelphia. So much for technology!

As a Cabin Service Director it is your responsibility to keep your crew in harmony. On a trip lasting 21 days it was always difficult keeping 15 people happy. On one particular trip I decided to organise a "cooking" experience between each galley. I asked the crew in each galley to cook a meal for me. This was such a huge laugh as the menus got better and better.

I was out shopping one day in Perth and found the crew of one galley coming out of the local supermarket after buying their groceries ready to cook on board. The first menu was an afternoon tea and they made up Rice Crispies with chocolate to make little cakes. Another meal was baked potatoes with various toppings. This was in the days before BA put such items on board.

The final menu was thought up by Carol Garland who was working in the upper deck galley. I was sitting in my little office downstairs and this aroma was wafting around. I went upstairs to investigate. There was Carol in a chefs' hat poaching pears in red wine in the hotcup, rolling out puff pastry with a wine bottle to make a gateau mille feuille and then making a pizza. She certainly got first prize. It certainly kept my crew together and there was so much rivalry to be the best galley.

6. How Things have Changed over the Years

I remember on my first flights on a DC3 Dakota these planes were not equipped with a PA system, therefore you would have to stand at the front on the aircraft in sight of all the passengers and do a "live performance." On one particular morning in Ostend (having done several round trips the day before and ending up having a nightstop in Ostend), I proudly said we would be taking off for Ostend. I felt so stupid as we were sitting on the tarmac in Ostend at the time.

I remember when we first started having films on board. Prior to this time all passengers would bring on newspapers, magazines, and books to read.

The first films were on big reels (which we knicknamed banjos) and were located in a hatrack in each cabin. When the film finished you would have to carry these big banjos down the cabin and replace them. Occasionally they would have a malfunction and come off of the reel and film would descend from the hatrack like spaghetti!

Nowadays it is so different with a huge selection of films, interactive games, news programmes, etc.

Prior to the in flight movie channels we used to hand out route maps which the flight crew would complete to show passengers our routing and the names of the crew members. Nowadays there is a moving map on the screen in front of you so you know exactly where you are.

Drinks and Meal Services on the B747

With the introduction of the larger aircraft it was deemed necessary to introduce bar trolleys and meal service trolleys. No longer would we go out and take a drink order and then deliver the drinks on nice little silver trays. Because weight was now a factor on these large aircraft, plastic glasses were introduced in the economy cabins.

The Cabins

When I first started flying for BOAC we only had two classes of cabin. First and Economy. The first changes came in with the B747. This aircraft had an upper deck lounge. It was a great job to be rostered in this position, which was affectionately called "The lounge lizard." You would serve drinks up there and sometimes play backgammon with the passengers. During the meal service you had to go downstairs and operate the microwave and generally help during the meal service. On night sectors, after dinner, passengers would sometimes try to race upstairs with blankets and lie down on the sofas. One had to quietly remind them this was a lounge and not a bedroom.

The company saw the need to have another class on the aircraft and this was called Club Class.

I remember the first aircraft I worked on after the first class cabin had seats fitted that converted in to beds. That really was the way to travel. Now there are beds in the Club cabin as well and another cabin has been introduced called "World Traveller Plus." The seats in this cabin are slightly wider and have a little more leg room than World Traveller (or economy as it used to be called).

One other thing that has changed is the fact that all cabins now have closed hatracks or overhead bins as they are now called. I can remember on one of the first trips when we had the closed racks one of the stewards lifted me up and I hid in the hatrack. He then asked one of the crew to put something in the hatrack and of course, there I was, and made them jump!

The Hotels We Stayed in

I have to say that apart from the rest houses in Bahrain and Karachi we were normally accommodated in first class hotels. Mind you, these have changed over the years. I can remember some of them didn't have air conditioning but quite often, just a large fan in the ceiling. In some places like Darwin life was not that comfortable. Neither did the crew transport have air conditioning. You would arrive at the airport like a damp rag having spent a while showering and doing your hair before departing the hotel for the airport.

7. Royal Flights

1974 – The Queens Flight

In 1974 I was chosen to fly with the Queen. This was to be one of the most fantastic experiences of my life. What an honour it was to be chosen to fly with the Queen. When I look back on my flying career I still feel that those couple of months were the most wonderful. I remember when I told my father that I wanted to be an air hostess – his reply was "a flying waitress." When I told him I was flying the Queen, he said he would take everything back that he had said previously.

We were flown out to Honolulu as passengers to await the arrival of Her Majesty. The day before, a meeting was held at our hotel which included all the cabin and flight crew, security personnel, the catering staff, engineers and ground staff. I seem to remember that the answer to every question that we posed was, "play it by ear."

We were due to go to Honolulu airport at 10 p.m. at night on the 28th January 1974. I can remember standing on the tarmac as the VC10 taxied round the corner with the royal standard flying out of the roof of the flight deck. We all stood there and were so proud as we stood to attention and couldn't believe that we would shortly be getting on that aircraft with "our Queen."

During our two months we took the Queen from Honolulu to Raratonga, from Singapore to Dubai, from Dubai back to Singapore and finally from Djarkata to Singapore.

The aircraft had been completely refitted inside. There was a small conference area, then a sitting room and dining area, and then five bedrooms. One for the Queen, Prince Phillip, Princess Anne and her then husband (Mark Phillips), and one for the late Lord Mountbatten. A dressing room with dressing tables and full length mirrors. The rest of the aircraft had first class seats fitted for her entourage. The galleys and toilets had all been carpeted. The special galley equipment included an electric frying pan and cut glass decanters. The Queen is extremely easy to please and eats quite simply. She carries her own bottled water with her.

For me it was a doubly exciting trip for me as Gordon Franklin CVO was one of the Queen's entourage – I had known Gordon since my Youth Club days.

When we arrived in Raratonga the Royal Party were carried away from the aircraft on platforms lifted by local people all wearing banana leaf skirts. As we stood on the aircraft steps after she had left it was quite exciting to see it as she was seeing it, being carried towards the thousands of cheering people.

The Queen had an evening to rest as she had flown all the way from London. Princess Anne and Mark Phillips had only joined the flight in Vancouver. However, we did feel sorry for the Queen as we found out the next morning that because she had slept so well on the aircraft she hadn't felt tired. Princess Anne and Mark Phillips were attending the opening of a school that evening and it is not like any normal mother/ daughter relationship because the Queen couldn't suddenly turn up with her daughter, so she was left back at Government House whilst we all went and enjoyed ourselves.

The next day the Queen left on an Air New Zealand aircraft to fly to Christchurch. We followed with the rest of her entourage. We had been invited to look at their aircraft just before the Queen arrived and we stood in line at the bottom of the Air New Zealand steps as she boarded.

The Government were brought down and the Queen had to come back to the UK in the middle of her trip. On the 28th February 1974 we took Her Majesty from Singapore to Dubai. After a few days in Dubai we were brought back to London and were then eventually flown out to Djarkata to take The Queen on her homeward journey from Djarkata to Singapore. My friend Gordon Franklin was just wonderful. He phoned me in the hotel and asked if I would like to visit the Royal Yacht Britannia that night. I wonder what you would have said. Of course, my answer was "yes." He also asked if any other members of

right and above:
The Queen being
carried off on
a special dias
carried by banana
leaf clad warriers.

my crew would like to join me. Well, I just blurted out "all of us" as I figured none of them would turn down an offer like this. The girls spent the afternoon in the hairdressers, we donned long dresses and went on the Royal Yacht for the evening. It was much smaller than I had imagined but a fantastic experience. In fact, we stayed so late I think Gordon was thinking he would have to order breakfast for us. Gordon gave me a powder compact with the Royal Yacht Britannia on it as a momento. I still have it to this day.

I have to say that that two months was the most exciting part of my 39 year flying career. It was quite a let down to have to go back to normal flights.

During my flying career I have carried quite a few members of the Royal Family, apart from those mentioned above I have also had the pleasure of serving or meeting the following:

Duke of Edinburgh
From Nairobi to London on 2nd October 1983

Prince William
I took Prince William to Nairobi (he was on a private visit) and it was the anniversary of his mother's death. What an absolutely charming young man he is. On my name badge was my MBE and he asked what I had received this for. More about this later in the book on the section about Dreamflight. But he did say that he had remembered his mother talking about my charity.

Prince William of Gloucester
On 2nd June 1970 I took Prince William of Gloucester from Honolulu to Fiji. I was working in first class and this was my very first meeting with a member of the Royal Family.

I was talking to his bodyguard about their onward travel arrangements. We were due to arrive in Fiji at 4 a.m in the morning. They apparently were going to take a private plane at 09.00. I said, almost as a throw away line, "well, we will be having a crew party as soon as we arrive at the hotel and you are both welcome to join us to fill in the time." Can you imagine the crew's surprise when they actually turned up to have a drink with us. The Captain said that he thought I was only joking when I said I had invited them. He was very sweet and had a couple of drinks and then left in the official car with a standard flying from the bonnet.

I did also meet him at a later date at an air show where I was doing some hosting in one of the hospitality tents, and I did get a chance to speak to him again. Sadly, Prince William was killed whilst piloting a light aircraft in an air race on 28th August 1972 near Wolverhampton.

Prince Tupouto of Tonga

On 28th May 1970 I had the pleasure of taking Prince Tupouto from New York to Los Angeles.

King and Queen of Tonga

From Bombay to Hong Kong 12th October 1983. The Queen of Tonga presented me with the bouquet that had been given to her on her departure from Singapore.

Princess Margaret

From Nairobi to Johannesburg on 1st September 1981. Imagine how thrilled I was when she asked to speak to me. My chief steward thought that I was in trouble, but my friend Gordon Franklin (who worked for the Queen) had asked Princess Margaret to pass on his regards to me! I certainly went up in the estimation of the crew.

Prince Andrew

I had the privilege of carrying Prince Andrew twice. The first time was from Singapore to Sydney. He is extremely easy to get on with and doesn't have any airs and graces about him at all. He comes in to the galley and meets all the crew. He asked me what I was going to do during my time off in Sydney. I explained that my brother and sister in law lived there and I would be going home to them.

About six weeks later I was to take him from London to San Fransisco. Imagine my surprise when he boarded, he asked me if I had had a good time with my family in Sydney. I later spoke to his bodyguard about this and he told me that HRH has an excellent memory. Prince Andrew was our only first class passenger on this particular day and he ended up showing me some of his family photographs on his laptop. At the time I was holding some questionnaires that I was just about to hand out to passengers on the aircraft. He asked me what they were for and I said to him "if you are not careful I will get you to fill one in." If he had of completed it, that would have been one questionnaire that I would not have handed in.

Prince Michael of Kent

In February 1968 I carried HRH Prince Michael of Kent from London to Nairobi via Khartoum and again in January 1969 from London to New York.

I was again to have the pleasure of looking after him London to Capetown. He was to be in Capetown for the departure of the Round the World Yacht Race. I will explain more about this later when we get to the fundraising section of Dreamflight.

Duchess of Kent

I brought the Duchess home from Capetown, she is a very quiet and private lady.

Duke of Bedford

From Seychelles to Mauritius on 9th Dec 1972

Other members of the Royal Family I have met but not on an aircraft are:

Prince Charles

I was privileged to be invited to the official opening of British Airways new Head Office at Waterside, near Heathrow Airport, in July 1998. I was to be in the Community Relations Department which deals with charities. I was personally introduced to him as were the other BA charities. I always remember in his official opening ceremony speech he said "it had been interesting touring the building and seeing the new concept of "hot desking." He carried on to say "I have heard of hot bunking before but not hot desking"! He certainly had us all laughing.

Princess Diana
Duchess of York
Earl and Countess of Spencer

8. Delays and Diversions

In the early days back in the sixties and seventies we had many more delays and diversions than happens nowadays. Far more fog around in November and we didn't have automatic landing features in those days. In fact, the first automatic landing I was on was in 1968, but it wasn't widely used then. Heathrow would often become fogbound around November time and diversions to Manchester and Birmingham would become the norm. It would be great fun in the bar in these hotels in the evening finding out how many other crews had been diverted and where they had come from.

Blackpool

On a VC10 when we couldn't land in Heathrow because of fog and Manchester was full of diverted aircraft, we had to divert to Blackpool. In those days the VC10 was a big aircraft and I don't think Blackpool had seen anything like it. They sent out double decker buses to collect the passengers. It looked so weird as normally there are only single decker coaches or buses.

I understand we made news in the local papers the next day.

USAF Base Masawa

On 21st February 1971 we were flying from Honolulu to Tokyo. We had already had to divert into Wake Island to get more fuel as we were suffering really bad headwinds on this particular day. We arrived over Tokyo and it was shrouded in thick fog. We circled for a while but eventually had to divert to a United States Air Force Base in the north east of Japan called Masawa.

When we arrived another BOAC flight flying from Anchorage

had also diverted. We waited for a few hours and the fog cleared in Tokyo but we were running out of hours as we had been on duty for such a long time. The Anchorage aircraft took off for Tokyo complete with our passengers and we stayed the night on the base. What great fun that was. We were housed in a "billet." There were 3,000 men on this base and suddenly 3 BOAC stewardesses turned up for the night! The Base Commander met us and we were cordially invited to the "Officers Mess" for drinks and these certainly flowed freely. Our Captain, Captain Jones had a slight limp and was nicknamed "Limpy Jones." After copious amounts of drinks one of the American Servicemen decided to ask "Limpy" how he got his limp. Well, the reply stunned us all. He told us "I was shot down on the last day of the war, by mistake, by the Americans!" Well, it all went very quiet and then someone shouted "buy them all another drink."

The next morning us girls had to go down the corridor to the ablutions (no en suite for us). The males on our crew decided to guard the door for us. I think that every door down the corridor had three mens' heads looking round to watch us proceed down the corridor.

We were invited to visit the Control Tower prior to our departure. Our captain decided to show them what our 707 was capable of doing (we had no passengers on board) and he told us to strap ourselves in securely. He said he wanted to show the Americans what our 707 could do as we had British Rolls Royce engines on our aircraft and not the Pratt & Witney type ones like the american airlines had. Well, we roared down the runway and he stood this 707 on its backside and we roared up like a rocket. So impressive. The fridge door in first class opened and a carton of milk rolled right down to the rear galley. We then came back and did a "beat up" of the runway and a waggle of our wings for the Americans and we were then on our way. Great excitement and something that just wouldn't happen these days.

Freeport

In June 1967 we were on our way from New York to Jamaica when Jamaican air traffic control went on strike. We ended up having to spend the night in Freeport in the Bahamas. We had the American film and television actor Van Johnson on board with us. We had great fun with our passengers in the hotel that night. I recently met up with the captain of that flight and he said he always remembered me as I organised a corridor party for all the passengers.

Entebbe

Due to fog in London we ended up being stuck in Entebbe for 3 days with our passengers in the same hotel.

When we did get airborne we had such a good relationship with our passengers that there were many laughs and jokes. We were due to operate to London via Zurich. We arrived in Zurich and our hold doors had frozen. It took a while for them to de-ice them and then we took off for London. Guess what, fog had descended on London once again, and we were diverted to Prestwick. Our passengers were absolutely brilliant I have to say. When we finally got airborne on the morning of the 7th January 1971 our passengers requested that if we had to divert again they should be allowed to choose the next place we would go to. Our captain was in agreement! However we safely landed back in London.

Dhaka

We were in the process of boarding the flight from Dhaka to London in February 2002 when it became apparent that one of our passengers had collapsed. We had a full flight and had almost completed the boarding process. Two of my crew were doing CPR and the defibrilator was brought in to use. A doctor was called for but the passenger was declared dead after 40 minutes.

A stretcher was brought on to take the passenger off the aircraft. I was discussing with the captain the best way to handle this. I felt that to take the body to the back of the aircraft and out of the rear door was not such a good idea as there was a bulkhead in the middle near the rear door. My plan was to take the Club World passengers on that side of the aircraft back to the Terminal and then bring the body on the stretcher to one of the forward doors.

You can imagine my horror when I went back into the cabin from the flight deck to arrange this, that the ground staff had already started to take the body towards the rear of the aircraft. I couldn't start shuttling this body backwards and forwards so I had to let them carry on. When the stretcher reached the back of the aircraft they had to lift and turn it almost vertical. My one worry was that the body would slide off the stretcher and through the open aircraft door. Fortunately, this didn't happen and I was mightily relieved.

I then had to deal with the four crew members who had been working so hard on this passenger and were obviously in a state of shock. I decided, with the captain's permission to delay the aircraft and take my four crew members off into the lounge to talk to them and order them some tea. After about 30 minutes they decided they wanted to operate the flight.

It was a very subdued crew that went about their duty on this day. Towards the end of the flight the captain had just put the seat belt signs on and we were preparing for landing when one of the crew came and said one of the passengers wanted to speak to me. I was almost at the point of annoyance as we had had a dreadful day and all I wanted to do was get on the ground and get the crew off the aircraft.

Anyway, out I went in to the cabin and was totally unprepared by what awaited me. I went back to sit at my seat for landing and was in tears. The crew member sitting beside me was most concerned. I said, "You are never going to believe this, but the passenger has written the most wonderful letter of thanks and had been round the whole aircraft and got all the other passengers to sign it." I quote

"We the passengers on British Airways flight BA144 from Dhaka, Bangladesh to London, on this day in February 2002 wish to express our most sincere gratitude, in very difficult circumstances, you performed your duties with an extraordinary level of professionalism and caring.
In an emergency situation you acted swiftly, with clear commitment and bravery, to do whatever you possibly could. When it was over, you took the best possible care of passengers, immediately resuming your other duties.

43

*British Airways should be proud to have you as crew and
we are grateful and honoured to fly with you."*

We were met by two of the Cabin Crew Management team and as soon
as we had said goodbye to our passengers they took us back to the
Crew Report Centre for a debrief. BA Managment were brilliant with
all of us that day.

Broken Ankle on Board

I was flying from Singapore to Perth in November 1971. All was quiet
on the aircraft and we were about an hour and a half out of Perth when
we hit really bad turbulence. I went down to the back of the aircraft
and there was this poor little old lady sitting on the toilet with her
knickers round her ankles and her ankle bone protruding through the
skin. She was so brave. Her husband was a doctor but he wasn't with
her on this particular trip. We made an announcement and one lady
came forward who was a nurse. We landed about an hour or so later
and she was taken straight to hospital. The crew visited her the next
day with a big bunch of flowers and we all signed her plaster.

Every time we hit turbulence after that (until the end of my flying
days), I was always very strict about making the passengers be seated
when the Fasten Seat Belt sign was on. So many of them would argue
with me, but I always say "if you have seen what I have seen you would
understand why I am so strict."

Instances like this are extremely rare, and if there are problems, the
crew are very well trained and capable.

9. Prominent People I have Met on Board

Over the length of my career I have met and carried some very famous people on the aircraft. I am listing a few below that you might be interested in.

ISOBEL BARNET (for those of you that can remember that far back). She used to be on the Quiz Show "What's my line".

DAVID FROST on many occasions when he was commuting between London and New York. First time October 1967 then again on 6th November 1969 London to New York and on many other occasions.

SIR ALEC DOUGLAS HUME February 1968 from Nairobi to Johannesburg.

LADY ASTOR from Nairobi to Mauritius.

THE REV DR DESMOND TUTU from Nairobi to Johannesburg. I will never forget, he was sitting in first class and was having trouble putting his seat back. Ever the attendant cabin crew member I went to help. Well, I pushed the back of the chair right back, the leg rest shot out and the poor Reverend's little legs shot in the air.

SIR OLIVER LEESE KCB, CBE, DSO (a British General during World War 11) from London to Entebbe on 29th December 1968.

PRESIDENT NYERERE of Tanzania from Rome to London but diverted to Manchester due to bad weather on 4th Jan 1969.

PAUL McCARTNEY from London to Nairobi on 9th November 1966.

SIR JACK BRABHAM (grand prix racing driver) from Frankfurt to Entebbe on 23rd Jan 1969 and from London to New York on 11th Feb 1970.

STIRLING MOSS (grand prix racing driver) from London to New York on 28th May 69.

ROY JENKINS (Labour Chancellor of the Exchequer) from New York to London on 12th Jan 1970.

LORD AND LADY CASEY (former governor General of Australia) from Darwin to Hong Kong.

SIR HUGH NORMAN-WALKER KCMG, OBE (Colonial Secretary of Hong Kong) from Bangkok to Tehran.

PRESIDENT LEE KUAN YEW of Singapore from Nairobi to Cairo on 13th September 1970.

HONOR BLACKMAN (English actress) from Barbados to Bermuda on 25th March 1971.

SPIKE MILLIGAN from London to Tehran on 5th October 1972.

LADY RAMSEY (widow of Sir Alf Ramsey) from New York to London on 4th June 1973.

KENNETH McKELLAR (Scottish singer) from Prestwick to New York on 21st Sep 1973. He was our only first class passenger and therefore instead of getting the trolleys out we were doing "silver service" for his meal. We had the tiny round roast potatoes, and yes, you guessed it, I dropped a couple straight in to his lap, and he was wearing a kilt. I offered to retrieve the said items and his reply was "not with that spoon and fork you don't, but you can use your hands!

Dr COGGAN (the Archbishop of Canterbury) from Singapore to Bombay in November 1976. Just after take-off we "lost" an engine and had to return to Singapore. I do hope the Archbishop didn't hear what I said! We went back to Singapore and had to stay the night before continuing our trip the next day.

JUNE WHITFIELD AND TERRY SCOTT (TV personalities) from Delhi to Hong Kong on 11th September 1977. They were great fun as we still had the lounge upstairs on the 747 in those days.

ANTHEA REDFERN (TV personality) from Barbados to London on 10th November 1980.

Dr DAVID OWEN (Politician) from London to New York on 6th November 1982.

LADY SOAMES (daughter of Sir Winston Churchill) from London to New York on 6th November 1982.

JULIE GOODYEAR MBE (Bet Lynch in Coronation Street) from London to Los Angeles on 15th November 1982.

MAURICE CHEVALIER from London to Los Angeles in November 1982.

JOAN ARMATRADING MBE (singer/songwriter) from London to Los Angeles on 15th November 1982.

ROBERT MORLEY CBE (actor) from Muscat to Singapore on 14th January 1983.

MAX BOYCE from New York to London in March 1984.

SIR MICHAEL PARKINSON CBE and LADY MARY (TV personality) from Abu Dhabi to London on 28th March 1984.

CLAUDETTE COLBERT (film actress) from London to Barbados on 17th November 1984.

LESLIE ASH (actress) from London to Barbados on 17th November 1984.

CLIFF THORBURN (Canadian world snooker champion) from London to Toronto on 31st March 1985.

CARLO PONTI (film producer and husband of Sophia Loren) London to Los Angeles on 23rd June 1985.

ROBERT CONRAD (American actor) from London to Los Angeles on 8th October 1985.

CHRIS BRASHER CBE (famous athlete) from London to New York on 30th October 1986.

STEVE CRAM MBE (famous athlete) from London to Chicago on 19th April 1987.

FANNY SUNNESON (famous for being Sir Nick Faldo's caddie) from Los Angeles to London on 12th November 1992. Fanny has become a friend and I am still in contact with her and see her at golf tournaments. She is now caddying for the Swedish golfer Henrik Stenson.

IAN WOOSNAM (golfer) Singapore to London 22nd February 1993 Unfortunately this is the end of my log book entries. I have certainly carried a huge amount more but sadly I never kept a record. Hindsight is a wonderful thing isn't it? I never imagined that I would be writing a book and could have used this information.

10. Interesting Places Visited

Some of you may be interested in reading about some of the places I have visited. I have put them in alphabetical order for you. Of course this is just a very few of the places that I visited over my 39 years in the air.

Anchorage – Alaska

I was always fascinated by Anchorage. We were always suffering big time changes here and in the summer it was difficult to sleep as it would only get dark for about an hour. I can remember one poor steward who was complaining about not sleeping. He had gone off and when it did get dark the rest of us were having a party so we decided to ring him and wake him so that he could see the dark!

Day trips out would be to Aleyaska stopping off at a bar called "The Bird's House." The place was covered with business cards from people from all corners of the earth.

Bangkok – Thailand

Bangkok for the girls was always a great shopping trip. I did do a trip to "The Bridge over the River Kwai." In the bar at the Amari hotel they had a brass bell and if anyone rang it they had to buy everyone a drink. A brass plaque was then put up on the wall. On my last trip (which was 20 months after I had retired) Craig Daly one of my Dreamflight crew rang the bell and then had my name put on the brass plaque. The crew wanted me to be remembered in Bangkok. I will leave you to have your own thoughts on that. A trip to Bangkok was not complete, especially if you had new crew members on your crew, until you had taken them down to Pat Pong and to the Queens Castle pub. I am not going to say any more about this.

Bahrain

We originally used to stay at the Gulf Aviation Rest house. Because we had generally done a long night sector either from London or from the Far East one feature on the menu was the "All day breakfast."

The Sheik would quite often invite the BA crews to his summer palace for a party. I only ever went once, as I didn't like having to wait until we were given the signal that we could leave.

Beirut – Lebanon

I remember on the flight to Beirut all the crew were saying that we meet in the Golden Bar which was right across the road from the Bristol Hotel where we stayed. I was really looking forward to going to this bar and imagined it as a long bar perhaps with marble counters and lots of "gold." Imagine my disappointment when I discovered it was a very small, dark, and dingy place and no sign of gold around at all! Great fun was had though and a little shop next door did wonderful corned beef rolls. In fact, we would sunbathe on the roof of the hotel and phone down to the shop, order our sandwiches, and they would pop over to the hotel and put them in the lift for us. We would then pay that evening when we went across to the bar.

Calcutta – India

We used to go to a local Club called the Tolly Gunge club and sunbathe all day. I have to admit that Calcutta was not a favourite of mine.

Cyprus

I was overruled by the Captain on one trip as I thought it would be a good idea if we all used the bycyles to go out for dinner one evening. The Captain said it would be OK getting there, but was of the opnion that it would not be such a good idea trying to get us all back when we had had copious amounts of wine.

Darwin – Queensland, Australia

Darwin is a very hot and humid place. We used to stay at the Fanny Bay hotel. This was a two storied building and as female crew were not allowed to stay in rooms on the ground floor we were always accommodated on the second floor. There were no lifts and no baggage porters in this hotel. Bearing in mind we were always on a three week trip, and therefore had heavy baggage, we were left to carry our suitcases up the stairs. In those days the suitcases didn't have wheels on them like they do now.

There was a lovely sign outside the bar which said, "thongs" (meaning flip flops) and vests will be worn after six. What a dress code?

Fiji
Was always a lovely place to visit. We would go out on a yacht called the Fletcher Christian. We would sail to an island and have a BBQ on the beach.

Georgetown – Guyana
We used to arrive here late at night. As the roads were dangerous, and there was the possibility of being hijacked, we had to travel in convoy with one stewardess in each car with three of the male crew members.

Harare – Zimbabwe
What a beautiful country and it saddens me now to see what is happening there. Trips to Victoria Falls and coming back on the overnight train. I also played a fair amount of golf in this country. They have marvellous golf courses. Dinner at Meikles Hotel was always a lovely experience.

Hong Kong
Was another favourite shopping trip. When I first started flying we stayed on Kowloon side. We used to go to the Mariners Club and then later we moved on to Hong Kong Island. A great thing to do was to catch the funicular to the top and see Hong Kong spread out at your feet. Great place to have a Pimms and just survey the scene before you. When the old airport Kai Tak was open you could see the aircraft landing and taking off. We were also made members of the Hong Kong Yacht Club and the restaurant in there was a great place to eat with

beautiful views of the harbour. Another favourite place was the China Fleet Club. We would also catch a bus across to the other side of the island to Stanley Market and then meet up in one of the bars for lunch and show each other our purchases.

Sometimes we would hire the junk boat the Jardalinka and sail around the harbour. I can remember sailing around the liner Queen Elizabeth who was lying on her side. She had been bought and was to be turned in to a floating University in Hong Kong but sadly that never happened.

Karachi – Pakistan

We stayed in a British Airways rest house (or BOAC as it was in those days.) It was literally ten minutes walk from the airport. We didn't receive any allowances here but everything was on the house. It was called Speedbird House but the Qantas crews nicknamed it Birdseed House. The rooms were very basic, just a bed, bedside table, and lamp and a shower shared with the room behind yours. You had to remember to lock the door so that the person on the other side didn't walk in on you. No air conditioning just a fan in the ceiling.

You were not allowed alcohol, but beer was available at the Rest House. The Qantas crews got round this though. The would bring a hose pipe with them. Why you ask? Well, they had a cork in each end and filled it with gin. Hence, 30 foot of gin!

The girls were always put down one corridor and this was nicknamed Virgin's Alley.

Moscow – Russia

I remember the first time I walked into my room in Moscow. The television in the corner of the room was almost the size of a caravan.

At the end of each corridor was a "dragon lady" keeping an eye on everything. Mind you, she would sell you tins of caviar for $10.

I was there for one New Years' Eve. The flight crew had arrived the day before us and so met us in the lobby when we arrived. They had booked a table for us at the celebrations in the Ballroom at the top of the hotel but these didn't comence till 23.00. As you can imagine a few glasses of wine had passed our lips by that time. Well, it was called wine, but tasted more like domestic disenfectant, but by the time you got to the fourth bottle it didn't seem too bad! We duly went upstairs and at midnight everyone stood up. We started letting off party poppers and streamers and singing Auld Lang Syne. We suddenly realised that everyone else around us was very silent and standing to attention!

Nairobi – Kenya

Nairobi was great for going on a safari to the Game Parks and latterly I would always play golf. We would always buy large baskets of fruit and flowers to bring home. It was great to visit the "Long Bar" which has been mentioned in many books about Nairobi. I was in a nightclub called The Sombrero Club one Christmas. There was an all black band and they were playing "White Christmas" it just seemed so funny.

New York – United States of America

I suppose over my 39 years of flying that New York would probably be my most visited city. It was always great for shopping. Visits to the Empire State Building and boat trips round the Island of Manhattan in the summer were always a favourite of mine. On one of my last visits there I finally managed to do the helicopter ride over Staten Island. I really wasn't comfortable in this mode of transport. I was put in the front as I was short and it was the type of helicopter that had a glass type bulb at the front. As I don't particularly like heights it was weird to look down through your feet and glimpse the streets of Manhattan. It was an education the first time that I went out for breakfast at Ansons (for my older flying friends who will remember this). I thought ordering breakfast was a simple thing to do until you encounter a New York waitress. To order eggs it would go something like this "scrambled, boiled, poached, griddled, fried – over easy, sunnyside up, well done, light", etc. and so it went on. Back in the sixties McAnn's was the place to meet up for lunch or sometimes evening meals.

Sydney – New South Wales, Australia

One of the most beautiful cities in the world. We used to get the ferry over to Manly Beach, and spend the day on this wonderful beach. At one time our hotel was at Bondi Beach. Sydney was one of my favourite places to visit not only because it was such a lovely place but my brother and his family were there and it was like going home for me every time I landed there.

Singapore

All crew members loved Singapore for the shopping. We used to meet up for lunch in the "Cellar Bar," everyone showing off what they had bought, same as Hong Kong.

The evenings would be an education. We used to go down to "Fatty's" restaurant. The word restaurant being used very loosely. You would sit outside on the pavement area. This would be followed by a trip to Bugis Street to see the transvestites all dressed up. Not to mention the rickshaw races back to the hotel.

Singapore is now such a different place. All modern gleaming shopping malls, but still a fabulous place to visit.

Trinidad

We stayed at an interesting hotel here. It was built on the side of a hill and was called "The Upside down Hilton." You walked in to Reception on the first floor and then went down to your rooms. We would also walk down to the Pelican Pub for lunch and evening meals. At the hotel they would have lovely parties and competitions out by the pool in the evenings and they would always love the BA crews being there as they would always be up for entering the "limbo" competitions. The crews would break the ice and then aother guests would join in.

11. Promotional Events for BOAC/BA

Over the span of my career I have been very fortunate and honoured that BA have used me for some of their promotional events.

One of the first, was when the company was still BOAC, and I was used for a photoshoot with a lot of the amenities that were on board for the children.

A few years later Pilkington glass brought out a range of sunglasses called Concorde. I was again priveleged to be at the promotion of these glasses.

In 1974/5 I was part of the recruitment team for BA. On occasions, between flying trips, we would go round the country and conduct interviews being held in hotels.

At various times I have been part of the meet and greet teams helping at events. One event was the Silver Spoon Awards at The Savoy hotel in London on 23rd November 1976 run by the Sunday Telegraph. As a stewardess we were used to bring out the various drinks and cooked items and some of the contestants were blindfolded and had to work out what the ingrediants were. At this event I met the Marchioness of Tavistock, she was Henrietta Tiarks and what a stunning lady she was. Some time later she was on one of my flights and after having slept all night, she still looked fantastic in the morning.

In March 1976 I was in a group of crew who were invited by Lord Balfor of Inchrye and Earl Amherst to visit the Palace of Westminster and have cocktails on the balcony overlooking the River Thames.

I had a very small non-speaking part in a film which was called

"The Games." It starred Charles Aznavour and Ryan O'Neal as an Olympic athelete. I had to play the part of a ground stewardess walking through the terminal and then play the part of a stewardess on board by delivering a drink. The amount of takes and retakes that those actors and actresses go through, I was really pleased to go back to my "normal job." The film was directed by Michael Winner.

I was featured in a double page spread in the Sunday Express on May14th 2006 (no, it wasn't Page 3 of "The Sun")! It was entitled the "High Life" and went through my life as a stewardess with BOAC plus girls from other airlines.

In recent years I have been asked to go on the Paul O'Grady show and talk about flying in the sixties. I went to the make up room at the same time as Paul himself. What a lovely man and he really puts you at your ease and is a good laugh as well.

I also played a small part in a CNN Business News report.

12. The End of My Flying Career

I was preparing for the end of my flying career and was due to retire at the end of July 2004. To be honest, I was looking forward to it. I think that 39 years in the air is a long time and I was looking forward to not having to spend nights out of bed and having to cope with time changes all year round.

Sadly, it didn't happen as I was planning. In March of 2004 I was diagnosed with cancer. A non-hodgkins lymphoma at the back of the stomach. I now faced nine months of intensive chemotherapy and therefore went on sick leave until my actual retirement date.

My consultant Professor Graham Smith at Frimley Park Hospital was just brilliant. Five times in the next nine months I would go neutropenic and would have to go back in to hospital on a drip for six days. This was not counting the days in hospital having the chemotherapy itself. During this time Professor Smith's secretary, Marie-Claude Willis, was so supportive and helpful to me. I can't thank the two of them enough and I am pleased to say they have both become firm friends of mine.

At the end of the chemotherapy Prof said I "had got through it". The only bad thing was just over a month later I had heart failure, back in the hospital for another two weeks. Thankfully, I got through that as well.

It was quite often normal practice to do a "last trip" to celebrate your years of flying. Because I had spent the last four months of my time with BA on sick leave I did not have a last trip.

Mike Street, who was a member of the Board promised me that when I was better I would have a last trip. So, twenty months after I had retired, Mike gave me a ticket, allowed me to choose my crew and my destination. I chose my Dreamflight crew and did a Bangkok/Sydney trip to see my family and my brother came back on the trip with me. Thank you Mike for all you did for me.

PART 2: The Story and History of Dreamflight

13. The History of Dreamflight

The Birth of Dreamflight

In 1983 I was on a committee of cabin crew at British Airways on a project called "Skyride." Cabin crews from all around the airline were raising money to charter an aircraft for a one hour long flight with underprivileged children on board for a Christmas party. The plan was for Santa Claus to pay a visit and give each child a present. As Heathrow was the largest airport the crews there chartered a Boeing 747 aircraft. The regional airports of Manchester, Birmingham, Glasgow, and Belfast chartered smaller aircraft.

In 1986 the Birmingham crews had not reached their target to charter their aircraft, so they asked the rest of us to fly our aircraft into Birmingham and take the children to see the "Disneyworld Road Show" that was touring the UK at the time. Can you imagine – 800 children all with twinkling headbands on as the lights were dimmed and the Disney characters performed their "magic." It was a fantastic sight. I was sitting with six children off of our B747 who were in wheelchairs. Their eyes were the size of saucers as they watched. A sight I will never ever forget.

It takes many people to get a Jumbo jet in the air, ground staff, engineers, cleaners, caterers, to name but a few, but it is only the flight and cabin crew that see the end result. For this reason we organised a party for all the staff involved after we returned to Heathrow. This was held in the BA Canteen at the Cranebank Training Centre. We had managed to obtain a video of the Road Show which we were able to show all the "ground staff" on our return. You know, when you have been involved in a day like this you are on a high – you have done something good and you then think – "what can we do next?" It was a throwaway line "Well, we have to go to Disneyworld itself!"

It is only when you wake up the next day and people start ringing up and asking "are you going to do it" that you begin to realise what you said the night before. My partner at the time, Derek Pereira, and I responded that we would think about it after Christmas. Well, we never stopped thinking about it and started to plan how we could achieve it. We also decided that we would like to take sick and disabled children and really give them their "Holiday of a Lifetime".

After the Christmas holiday and after we had written down all the pros and cons, we went to see the Doctor at the British Airways Medical Centre and put our idea to him. He felt that we would be opening up "a can of worms" but he would put our idea to Sir Colin Marshall the Chief Executive of British Airways. Meanwhile we had been talking to friends about how we could set up fundraising etc. We had approached the Chartridge Training Centre near where we lived and they were willing to help with raising funds. A few days later the doctor telephoned to say that the answer was "no" but if we really wanted to persevere with the project we would have to make an appointment to see Sir Colin ourselves.

With no more ado, I rang and made an appointment which was to be the day after we had run a Ball for the 747 Golf Society – something else that I had been instrumental in starting!

At the appointed time we sat outside Sir Colin's office, feeling tired from the Ball the night before, and quite nervous about this meeting. Sir Colin was just marvellous. He made us outline our plans and when we mentioned Chartridge his response was, "yes, I know about this" so he had obviously done his homework on us! Towards the end of the meeting he asked if we knew what we were doing. What a question, of course we knew what we were doing, but we were wrong, and I did admit this to him some ten years later. Our plan was for this to be a one off trip to Orlando. In 2011 Dreamflight celebrates its' 25th Anniversary. Sir Colin was right, he knew it would not stop at just one trip. He gave us his blessing and asked to be kept updated and accepted our offer to become President.

It was an enormous task to set up and the first thing was to choose a name. After much deliberation we settled on the name DREAMFLIGHT – quite aptly named don't you think? A logo had to be produced and headed notepaper, etc. In those days all the typing was done on my IBM golf ball typewriter. We didn't possess a computer as they were fairly new then. However, my brother worked for IBM in Sydney and he persuaded IBM to donate a computer. When I think back to that funny little computer which I think must have been steam driven, I have to laugh. IBM telephoned to say they were happy to donate the hardware but couldn't donate any software. I didn't know the difference, so politely accepted their very kind offer. I thought you just had to switch it on and it would be like an electric typewriter. My goodness, how I have learned over the years. I was terrified of this computer in case I wiped out all the work that we had done.

We then contacted a consultant paedriatian at Stoke Mandeville Hospital and his wife who was a nurse there. They in turn contacted doctors, nurses, and physiotherapists around the country asking for volunteers to come and help on the trip together with getting nominations of children. We had put an advert in the British Airways News asking staff to back us and not only offer help but also help with the fundraising. We called on all our friends and relatives and everyone was so helpful.

I spent nearly every hour I had working on Dreamflight. My mother would come and do the housework to relieve me of the task, and to do a lot of the menial tasks like licking, sticking, and stapling all the mountain of paperwork that had to be sent out. We would quite often eat in the village pub "The Pheasant at Ballinger" in Buckinghamshire and have meetings there as there was no time to go food shopping or do any cooking. Pat & Nigel Wimpenny-Smith, the landlord and his wife, were, and still are, great supporters of Dreamflight.

Some neighbours, Michelle and Marcus Patte-Dobbs – Michele was a nurse, who had previously taken small groups of sick children away, were so helpful in giving us ideas on how to set the trip up, and, in fact, they came on the first few trips with us.

The paperwork alone on this project was a huge mountain. Not only did we have to find all the medical staff, other escorts, and the 288 children, we had to ensure that everyone had a passport and it was in the days when you needed a visa to visit America. We had to arrange transport for the children to get to Heathrow Airport. We flew groups of children from Belfast, Newcastle, Edinburgh, Glasgow, Manchester, Birmingham, and we coached them in from South Wales and the West Country.

For those coming from long distances we had to arrange hotel accommodation the night before the flight. This was to be at the Penta Hotel (now the Renaissance) at Heathrow, and the rest of the group would be brought to the hotel by their parents on the Monday morning. We had to arrange for everyone to be taken to the British Airways hangar where the specially chartered aircraft would await with "Dreamflight" on the side of it.

In the middle of all this, we had to go to Orlando to set the trip up on that side of the Atlantic. We went and stayed at the Howard Johnson hotel on Kirkman Road (now called the Holiday Inn) and this is where we still stay today. We had to book their banqueting rooms to arrange for breakfast and dinner. We had to arrange for thirteen buses and we had meetings with our British Airways Manager in Orlando, Peter Heller. Peter, we owe you a great vote of thanks for setting up procedures that are still very much in practice today. Peter arranged for the aircraft to be able to go to the private jet area of Orlando airport and not to the main terminal. This meant that we could have the buses waiting on the tarmac and the children could disembark straight down the steps and on to the waiting buses. Peter also contacted the Immigration Officials and arranged for an immigration officer to come to London and then fly back with us and complete all the immigration procedures on board. This saved so much time and some immigration officers, Maria Perez and Michael Haggerty, have become firm friends and still come and help the children on their days off whilst we are going round the theme parks.

The Orlando Police became involved and offered to give us a police escort to the hotel. This still happens today and every year we seem to get increasingly more police bikes. When we are ready to leave the

left: This is the motorcade of buses – a total of 13 Mears buses.

airport they close the I4 (which is equivalent to our M25) and off we go to the hotel with flashing lights and sirens. Pretty impressive. They also escort us back to the airport on our departure.

The original plan was to fly to Orlando on the Monday, go to Magic Kingdom on Tuesday and Wednesday, and then depart Thursday evening back to London. Whilst we were on the "set up trip" Seaworld contacted us and invited us to take the children to their park. This was then scheduled for the Thursday and we would go direct from Seaworld to the airport for the return flight. We got caught in a huge downpour of rain and we got soaked, so on the aircraft coming home we had childrens' trainers in the ovens trying to dry them out!

We also arranged to have groups of American volunteers come and join us to help. There again, some of these wonderful people who came along that first year are still with us today (2012) and are true Dreamflighters.

Back to the UK and more and more paperwork and arrangements to be made. The Police at Heathrow became involved and arranged a police escort to take us from the hotel to the hangar. This is a group of policemen from the Queens Special Escort Group (SEG).

Meanwhile, we had to set up a huge fundraising programme to fund the trip. Our first port of call was to British Airways News, to ask them to put an article in the BA News asking the staff of BA to support us. We needed their help not only to fundraise but needed offers of help in the various areas of the country and we also needed help to do "an off airport" check in at the hotel to save us having to go to the terminal. We needed check-in staff and baggage handlers at the hotel. There again another procedure was set up that is still in practice today. I can't thank all of these volunteers enough. I do appreciate their help.

We had to charter the aircraft, arrange the ground handling, and the catering. Mike Street was Head of Catering Services (later to become a Board member) and a true supporter of Dreamflight to this day even after his retirement. Mike admitted to me years later that when he offered to give us the catering for free, he thought, "She will never get that project off the ground, so I will just humour her!"

We then thought it would be a good idea to send a small team of people to Orlando to arrange the hotel check-in before we arrived. Two BA Managers, Penny Heard and John Ackland offered to do this for us.

The BBC contacted us as they were running a documentary programme called Forty Minutes and they came along to do a feature film of the trip. The documentary was called "Five go to Florida." They seemed to forget that we had another 283 children on the flight!

I then contacted a very dear friend of mine, Gordon Franklin. Gordon I had met when I was in my teens doing youth club work. Gordon worked at Buckingham Palace and I had been on a royal flight with him, and I was now asking him how I could invite HRH Princess Diana to see the flight off. He told me who to write to and asked me to send the letter to him so that he could make sure it went to the right place, and also put in a good word for us. Can you imagine our excitement when she accepted the offer and not only that, the Duchess of York would greet us on our return. This caused another frenzy of meetings as security had now rocketed. We had to have a plan of action in the hangar. All the top brass of BA would have to be invited to the departure including Lord King who was Chairman of the company. Ron Scobling who was in charge of special events in BA, was a tremendous help in setting up all the departure arrangements.

My life that year was totally consumed by Dreamflight.

above: Patricia taking Princess Diana in to the hangar to greet some of the children. Lord King is just behind us.

above: The Duchess of York came on board to welcome the children home when we landed at Heathrow on our return.

The First Dreamflight

The day started at 05.45 (mind you we had not slept much during the night!) as we were due to do two live interviews on breakfast time TV. This was all arranged in the hotel.

The children began to check-in and the stars started to arrive to meet the children. These included Bobby Moore, Steve Davis, Rolf Harris, Roy Castle, Pete Murray, Liz Frazer, Michael Strachan, Floella Benjamin, The Bucks Fizz group, and Jimmy Tarbuck.

We had Princess Diana arriving at 12.00 to meet the children and wave us off at 13.00. Thankfully it all proved to be "organised" chaos and all was reasonably calm by the time HRH arrived. We managed to get everyone transported from the hotel to the specially converted hangar. It was so wonderful to pull round to the side of the hangar and see the aircraft there with DREAMFLIGHT painted on the side. Something that still happens today. There was also the castle over the bottom of the steps. This was a present from our friends in the Engineering Department who had built it. We still use the same castle today.

I had planned to go on board the aircraft and change in to a clean uniform and "top up" my make-up before Princess Diana arrived. But, all of a sudden, one of the BA staff said "get on the red carpet Pat, as HRH is just about to arrive." We stood with Lord King and Sir Colin Marshall awaiting her arrival and our presentations to her. She totally took my breath away, and I almost forgot to curtsey, as she said "Good morning, I was watching you on television whilst I was getting ready at Windsor Castle." Well, you could have knocked me over with a feather. It is usually the other way round and I would have been watching her on the televison.

It was planned that half the children would have been pre-boarded on the aircraft. I escorted her to meet the other half of the children who were still in the hangar. I then walked her out to the aircraft and whilst she was touring the back section of the aircraft and meeting the children that had been pre-boarded, we had to quickly load the rest of the children. When everyone was on board, we escorted HRH off the aircraft and said goodbye to her at the bottom of the steps. It was a quick dash back on board, closed the doors and then she waved us off. I was looking through the windows and she was standing next to my Mum.

On our arrival in Orlando we were met by the Orange County Police Sheriff's office. Police outriders met the aircraft at the end of the runway and escorted us to the private ramp at Orlando Airport. We did not go to the main terminal.

A British Airways spokesman stated later "The idea of a jumbo 747 being escorted by motorcycles was very unusual, but Dreamflight itself was, and still is, very unusual.

A quote I have taken from the publication from the Sheriffs' office. "Cpl Richard Bates clocked the aircraft doing a speed of 120 knots during it's landing rollout but (in another first) was talked out of writing a citation by the plane's pilot."

Dreamflight 1988

Having said that Dreamflight 1987 was to be a one-off trip everyone convinced us that we could not end it there. It was decided to do a smaller trip in 1988 travelling on BA's scheduled service flight from Gatwick.

The trip was planned with 82 children plus the accompanying medical team and escorts. We all met at the Heathrow Hotel on Sunday 13th November. Very sadly we had to leave with only 81 children as one of the children sadly died two weeks before the trip. Nowadays we have a standby system and have put a child on the trip only the day before departure.

On the morning of departure we had the dreaded phone call, and Sir Colin popped in to see us to advise us that the flight was possibly going to be delayed. After a short delay we then made our way down to Gatwick Airport. The scheduled flight those days went via Manchester. All was fine until we landed in Manchester and the aircraft developed a technical problem. I immediately got off the aircraft and with the help of the Manchester ground staff managed to secure 125 rooms in

Blackpool (there were no rooms available in Manchester) should we have to stay the night. One of the things you have to do when you are in charge of a project like Dreamflight is to be able to be one jump ahead. Three and half hours later and just before the crew were due to go out of hours, we took off for the nine hour flight.

This particular year we added Epcot and the Kennedy Space Centre to our schedule. We also went to a dinner show called King Henry's Feast.

On our last day in Florida we organised a swimming gala in the hotel swimming pool and a BBQ. Whilst all this was going on I received the dreadful news that the flight back to London was delayed by 10 hours. Swing into action again and think of a back-up plan. Pick up was going to be 4 a.m. in the morning. We decided to put all the children to bed in their Dreamflight track suits so that in the morning we just needed to brush their teeth and be on our way.

On the flight back one of the passengers organised a collection and presented us with a cowboy hat full of money.

We arrived back at Gatwick Airport at 11 p.m. and the crew who had flown us on our outbound flight had turned up to welcome us back and lend a hand. Because quite a few of the children couldn't get home from Gatwick that night we booked rooms at the Crest hotel and so the trip carried on. Next morning we coached everyone up to Heathrow to get their flights to Edinburgh/Glasgow/Belfast/Newcastle, etc.

Dreamflight 1990

For Dreamflight 1990 we decided there would be three "small" Dreamflight trips one week after the other using BA's scheduled service flights again. I flew out on the first flight as supernumerary crew, came back at the end of the week, saw the second trip off, then met the first trip back in to Gatwick, and then flew out on the third trip. I have to say, on reflection, it was very tiring. My mother went out for all three weeks and kept an eye on things when I wasn't there.

On the first flight there was one lady passenger who was not best pleased at seeing this large group of children embark. She did not like BA, and did not like Dreamflight. Well, that was a challenge. As I was working as supernemary crew, I was in my cabin crew uniform. Having been told about this lady I felt I had to go and have a chat with her and give her a leaflet. Whilst I was explaining that all these children had something wrong with them, they didn't have any parents with them but all the adults were doctors, nurses, physiotherapists, etc. who were all donating their time, her eyes started welling up, and she apologised to me. At the end of the flight she handed me an envelope with a donation in it. And, yes, you have guessed, she will fly BA again!

Dreamflights 2004/2005/2009

Most years run quite smoothly but as with any big project there are going to be years that are more problematic than others. Here I will detail some of the years that challenged us.

2004

The only year I have not managed to travel on the trip as I was going through intense chemotherapy for my cancer at the time and was back in hospital. There I was, lying in hospital with a drip in my arm and not realising what was going on at Heathrow Airport!

Mike Street one of the Directors of British Airways had phoned me from the hangar to let me know how things were going. John Tye (one of our Trustees) had telephoned me from the flight deck of the aircraft as they were being towed from the hangar. I spent the afternoon thinking about them enjoying their flight. I thought about them around tea time and of course on their landing time.

Can you imagine the next day when Neil Parsons, one of the cabin crew, texted me to say, "you have obviously heard about yesterday by now." Well, I hadn't. I imemdiately phoned Mike's PA and said to Tricia "What happened yesterday?" She stuttered a couple of times and then said, "You had better speak to Mike himself." He admitted to me that the flight had developed a technical problem and had had to taxi back to the hangar. The fault couldn't be fixed and they had to do an aircraft change. This necessitated another aircraft being brought over alongside the Dreamflight aeroplane and all the luggage, catering and of course the passengers be transferred. They took off some six hours late. Mike said to me "we didn't dare phone you because we know that drip would have been pulled out of your arm and you would have been up to the airport to help sort things out."

I now had my Professor on strict instructions to get me well enough to be discharged from hospital and be able to be at Heathrow to greet them all back. Professor Graham Smith, I owe you a lot and I am so pleased to have you as a personal friend. You got me well enough to be there for that arrival and you got me through my cancer. You saved my life. You are a very special person in my life.

Apparently one of the children was overheard to say, "because we lost 6 hours at the start of the holiday, are we going to stay an extra 6 hours at the end?"

Another child said after sitting on the ground for three hours at Heathrow, "my ears hurt with this flying, do yours?" Bless him, they hadn't even taken off.

2005

This was the year after my cancer treatment and I returned absolutely more determined than ever to make sure these children had the time of their young lives. I particularly went to talk to the young girls who were going through cancer treatment and had lost their hair. It was different for me when I lost mine, I was a lot older, but for a young teenage girl it must be more traumatic. I spoke to one young girl whose hair was just coming back and was very thin and spikey. She had gelled it so that it stood up and I told her that it looked great and that I knew exactly how she felt as I had been through it myself. On the day that we went to Discovery Cove and she came out of the water and her hair was all flat, I said to her "having a bad hair day then", her reply to me was "Pat, only you could say that to me with such feeling." It has given me a special bond with these young girls.

I still feel, 25 years later, that these children who go through so much, deserve a treat in life.

2009

Dreamflight 2009 proved to be quite a challenge. In fact, I said it was the hardest year since the setting up of the charity in 1987.

It was the year of the swine flu epidemic, so we knew it was probably going to be quite difficult. Dr Simon Bailey, our Medical Director, had managed to get a large amount of Tamiflu donated to take with us. I would add at this stage I don't think we did get any cases of it.

We also learned that one of our helpers was unable to come which meant that we had to set up a merchandise team to sort out the merchandise on the day of departure and bag up all the groups children's clothing. This being the T shirts and track suits that they would all be wearing to travel in. We also had to sort out our entertainment team.

Then the bombshell was dropped just four weeks before the trip. I received a phone call from the hotel we stay at in Orlando to say the wing we usually stayed in had been closed down.

I immediately made plans to do an emergency trip over there and to take two of our trusted helpers with me. Jo James and Lilian Eckford always go over a few days before our arrival and sort out all the allocation of rooms and then check us all in and get the keys and envelope them up prior to our arrival. I have to say, I could not have sorted all this out without them.

The hotel had another wing but it is made up of suites. We therefore could not accommodate everyone in the hotel. The hotel had moved other guests who had been booked in to the suites to other hotels, so that we could have the complete wing. We managed to accommodate all the children and their immediate escorts in the new wing. It resulted in approximately 60 helpers having to stay in the hotel across the road. Not ideal but it was workable. The aircraft operating crew, the night nurses, our American helpers, and most of our video team were accommodated in the other hotel. The poor crew had to be up before 6 a.m. to come over to our hotel to do "pool duty" a sort of lifeguard duty every morning.

Just 48 hours before the trip, when you think that nothing else can go wrong, I received a phone call from my friend Robin Hayes (who organises the Regimental Band of the Royal Welsh) to tell me that the Ministry of Defence had pulled the plug on all outside events for the band. This was a great disappointment as the Band has supported us since the very beginning and are a great part of the Dreamflight Experience for the children. They not only play at the party the night before but also march all the children out from the hangar to the aircraft. We had also paid out over £1800 for their hotel rooms and the coach up from Wales. Everyone has always said that my networking is second to none, and that my address book would fetch hundreds of pounds. I had not realised how good it could get until that morning! The local Conservative MP has an office just opposite the Dreamflight Office. I popped into see her secretary and said that I felt we needed some help. She told me to send an email to Cheryl Gillan and she would phone her and ask her to look at her emails as she was in parliament that day.

Cheryl, bless her, phoned me to say this should not be happening to us with all the good work we were doing. She then informed me that she had recently been made Shadow Secretary of State for Wales. What a stroke of luck. Cheryl managed to get it taken to cabinet level and the end result was we got our band. Mind you, this was with help from the Band themselves as well, as they were so disappointed.

I owe a great debt of gratitude to everyone for working so hard to make it all work this particular year. We did have more than our fair share of coughs and sniffles amongst both the children and the adults. There was one day when we decided that one complete group, and one or to others from other groups, should not go to the water park as we didn't think they should be in the water all day. Thinking whilst on the run, it was decided that I would take this group to Disney Quest (a building full of computer games) but unfortunately the tickets could not be transferred. So I went complete with credit card to purchase 36 tickets for this group. I then arranged for someone to come and collect me and take me to Blizzard Beach and look after the large group again.

Jason Beamish-Knight, in the entertainment team, was brilliant. He offered to stay back at the hotel ready for when this small group came back, and he set up films and games for them in the dining room. This was Dreamflight at it's best, everyone working to make sure things happen. The children were all unaware of the problems we were facing, which is the main thing.

At the group leaders meeting on the last night there were over 20 of us sitting round the table and I think absolutely everyone was coughing.

On arrival back into London, from my point of view, it is always a huge relief to stand on the steps of the aircraft and put both thumbs up to show everyone that it has been a great trip and we are all safely home. For 2009 you have no idea of the relief that I felt.

14. Trip Format and Achievements of the Children

Over the years and after many hours of thought, we have now settled on a format that seems to work very well. We now take 192 children split in to 12 groups from Scotland, Wales, Northern Ireland, and all over the UK. The basic format is still the same with a group leader in charge, one doctor, three nurses, one physiotherapist, and three non-medical escorts in each group. All escorts, apart from the Group Leader, is responsible for two children. For me it is wonderful that these people from the medical profession take time out from their very demanding jobs to be volunteers on Dreamflight. Without the medical staff Dreamflight would not be possible.

We also take a team of night nurses, entertainers, admin team, and of course our very important video team and a photographer. Every child will receive a video (or should I say DVD now) of their holiday, and a DVD of still photographs. At least the parents can see what their children have got up to whilst away.

The first trip was only five days but these days the trip has been extended and it is now a 10 day trip. Although we have made changes to the itinerary over the years and tried different things, we have now settled on a basic format that seems to work well.

In the past we have included trips to Cape Kennedy, but the little girls aren't really interested, and most children do not like to be on the coaches for too long. We have also visited Epcot, Fort Wilderness, and

Animal Kingdom. On a couple of years we have had to go to Typhoon Lagoon when Blizzard Beach has been closed for refurbishment.

At one time we used to go to an evening show called Wild Bills. It was basically a cowboy show and the children loved it. On one of the first trips I needed to pay around $6,000 in travellers cheques to the establishment for all of our dinners. Well, somehow or other, I forgot to take the travellers cheques with me. So, in effect, we had walked out without paying for 420 dinner tickets. Alan Findlay who was in charge of Wild Bills did forgive me and we are still friends today. Thank goodness in these days of technology we can organise payment electronically. Alan is now at Championsgate Golf Complex.

We went to King Henry's Feast for a couple of years and then another dinner show we went to for a few years was Dolly Partons' Dixie Stampede. This was a very similar experience to Wild Bills but involved a horse stampede. A gentleman called John Stine, who was the Manager of Dixie Stampede, invited us to come to the show at no charge. How generous is that, 420 dinner tickets. I had met John at a golf day years earlier when he worked for Universal Studios. John and I had played in the same team and have always remained friends. Dixie Stampede has now closed down but John is working at Cape Kennedy and is hopefully going to get an astronaut to come and talk to the children this year.

It is always so nice to see the children bonding on the trip. Two children share a bedroom and we always make sure that if a child is wheelchair bound then they have to share a room with another child who is ambulant so that they can get to the phone at night if necessary. About the third day of the trip, you will start to see the ambulant child pushing his buddy in a wheelchair into the breakfast room rather than the adult escort pushing the child. Mind you, sometimes they are trying to do "wheelies" with them.

The day will quite often start at 6 a.m. with quite a large percentage of the children going swimming. A good deal of physio work also takes place in the pool. Our aircraft crew are rostered "Pool Duty" and act as lifeguards. Those that don't want to swim will probably stay in bed until 7 a.m. Everyone is then down to breakfast and ready to board the buses by 9 a.m and it is off to the theme parks for the day. A large amount of the children will swim when we arrive back at the hotel, so the crew are back on "Pool Duty"

This is a typical itinerary.

Saturday   – Hotel at Heathrow for check-in and party
Sunday   – Flight to Orlando
Monday   – Magic Kingdom
Tuesday   – Universal Studios
Wednesday   – SeaWorld
Thursday   – Blizzard Beach – a water park
Friday   – Islands of Adventure
Saturday   – Hollywood Studios
Sunday   – Discovery Cove
Monday   – Police & Fire Display and Shopping Malls

Our first visit to Discovery Cove was in 2005. Seaworld invited us to go and visit as they wanted to experiment with a large group. They very kindly said that as we were such an organised large group they wanted to do a trial with us. They have even made special matting to put on the sand to make it easier to pull our wheelchairs on.

As this is the last day of the trip and the adults have got to know their children and become very close to them, there are a lot of tears from the adults as they see their special charge swimming with a dolphin.

The flight home is so different from the flight out. Everyone is very tired on the way home and the children are curled up with their heads in the escorts laps. It is wonderful to walk round the aircraft during the night and see them all.

Prior to the trip, so that the children can get to know one another, each group leader will organise a pre-trip meeting in their area. It is so good for a child to meet the other child that they will be sharing a room with and an opportunity for the parents to meet the escort who will be responsible for their child during the holiday. It also gives the group doctor and the nurses an opportunity to discuss medical conditions and treatments with the parents. It also dispels many of the concerns the parents may have had.

Each group leader will also arrange a post trip meeting a few months after the trip. It is amazing how quickly the children will get back in to "Dreamflight mode." I was at one reunion when a child asked her escort to take her to the toilet even though her parents were there! It is a rule on Dreamflight that no child must go to a public toilet at the theme parks, etc. without being escorted.

For the adults, about six weeks before the trip we organise a briefing day and we utilise the British Airways Training Centre near Heathrow. This is a day for the adults to get to know one another and a chance for myself, the Medical Director, the other trustees and other key people in Dreamflight to impart useful information about the trip, and, to make them aware of our expectations for the fulfilment of their role.

The Groups and Escorts

I have explained about the make-up of the groups i.e. a group leader, doctor, 3 nurses, 1 physiotherapist, and three non-medical escorts. The non-medical people have usually earnt their place to be on the trip. The group leader is able to choose one non-medic and the Trustees will then allocate a further two non-medics. The majority of non-medics have raised a considerable amount of money and we want them to be able to see how their money is being spent. Sometimes a company has donated a large sum and we offer them a place for a member of their staff. In this way, they can go back and write in their Companys' newsletters about their Dreamflight experience. Non-medics may be invited back for a second year but will then be expected to take a year out. This doesn't mean they will never go again but with so few places we do have to rotate and bring in new supporters as well.

There are 12 groups from all areas of England, Ireland, Scotland, and Wales. There are nine adults and 16 children per group.

The groups are named after theme park characters and the name is chosen by the group leader.

Selection Process for the Children

We have what we call a nomination form which really is like a medical questionnaire. This has to be completed by the child's doctor. The forms are sent out at around the end of January every year. The forms are returned to the group leader who will generally sit down with their group doctor and initially go through the nomination forms. Around 28 per group will be sent to our Medical Director, Dr. Simon Bailey, who will then make the final selection. We have to ensure that the child will be capable of making the trip and that we have the correct equipment etc to make their trip a safe and pleasurable experience.

The letters of invitation are posted out around June/July time. The office then becomes very busy as a great deal of forms need to be completed by the parents or guardians and then all the information has to be entered on to the computer. We not only need all the medical information we need the childens' sizes so that we can order Dreamflight track suits and T shirts ready to be issued for them to travel in.

Night Nurses

We have a group of six night nurses who will be on duty every night in the hotel. They fly to Orlando three days ahead of us so that they are well rested and ready to begin their night shifts as soon as we arrive. The night shift is a very important part of Dreamflight.

Et Group

This group is the largest group on Dreamflight and doesn't even have any children in it. Mind you, I sometimes begin to wonder! This group comprises all the adults who are on the trip who do not have direct responsibility for a child in a group. This includes people like myself, the Medical Director and other trustees, the floating nurses, the floating doctor, the entertainment team, the video team, our photographer, our admin team and the night nurses. It is usually in excess of 30 people.

I would like to tell you about two adults who got involved with

Dreamflight because their children were originally invited to come with us. They started off by fundraising for us and then subsequently have been on the trip as escorts.

Malcolm Smith's son Tony came on the trip quite a few years ago and Malcolm initially joined us as an escort and has now been a group leader for a while. Tony now works for British Airways as check-in staff and is always there to check Dreamflight in these days.

Diane Cox's son Peter came with us and the same as Malcolm, Di started fundraising for us and then came as an escort. I print here a piece that Di wrote in the Dreamflight newsletter in 2006.

"What words best describe my trip to Florida with Dreamflight. – awesome, amazing, magical, humbling?"

In 1999 my son Peter was invited to take part in a "trip of a lifetime". The excitement which was generated was amazing, but I felt apprehensive – my son out of the country, thousands of miles away and most of all ... without me!

I remember standing in the hangar for the return, waiting for the sight of his face and when I did catch a glimpse of him – relief, that he was back in one piece. He got the biggest cuddle ever and all I got was "Oh mum, stop it."

Days and weeks afterwards there was a kind of glow around him, I couldn't put my finger on what was different but something was. Perhaps he had returned with some Disney magic.

When I received a letter from Pat Pearce asking me to be an escort on the 20th Dreamflight, I felt extremely honoured and decided there and then that the children in my care would also have their "trip of a lifetime" whatever it took.

From the moment I went to get my two boys up in the morning, the fun would begin. On the coach everyone would be telling jokes, singing and this continued throughout the day. Each day melted into the next, smiles and laughter, amazement and achievements were always the order of the day.

Seeing their parents faces in the hangar, my feelings from 1999 came flooding back – is my child OK did he miss me, were

*there any problems? My reply was that they didn't have any time
for anything except fun and laughter.*

Thank you Di. Sadly Diane's Peter lost his battle for life but Di has
been a stalwart supporter of Dreamflight and fundraised for us over
the years.

Overseas Children

Over the years we have taken quite a few children from overseas and
I would like to explain the reasons for this.

Hong Kong

A fellow crew member friend of mine, Gillian Conway, had decided
to help me fundraise. Her father was the secretary of the Hong Kong
Cricket Club at the time and she enlisted his help. He decided to
organise a fundraising aerobathon and many of the members joined
in. When the money was raised we flew out to Hong Kong for a dinner
to receive the cheque. We decided on the spot, that as these people
had so kindly raised all this money for us and wouldn't see how their
money was being spent, we would take four children from Hong Kong,
together with nurses, and they could have their own mini departure.
To this day we still take two children from Hong Kong. They fly in a
couple of days before we are due to go to Orlando, so that they can get
over their jet lag, and can also see a little of London.

One lady who was at the dinner I had met in the UK years earlier.
Hazel and her husband Ray Corstin, were at the presentation dinner
when we decided to take the Hong Kong children, Ray said, that as he
worked for Cathay Pacific Airways he would get complimentary tickets
for them. How nice of Cathay to support us.

Nowadays they fly in with British Airways but the fundraising still
goes on there under the leadership of Gill Wright. They still organise
fundraising events and host a "Bon Voyage" party for the children.

Chernyobyl

One of our Scottish Dreamflight stewardesses who had organised a fundraising ball in Scotland also worked very closely with the Chernobyl Trust charity. They would bring children from Chernobyl for a month's holiday in the UK staying with British families. For many years we took a couple of the children that were staying in the UK with us on Dreamflight. It is amazing that children don't seem to have any language barriers at all.

Rest of the World

Because we are supported so much by BA staff and fundraising has gone on all around the world for us over the years we have taken children from:

Sydney
Perth
Auckland
Zimbabwe
Nairobi
Bahrain

It does tend to become a logistical nightmare making all the extra travel arrangements and organising medical staff to travel with them so most of the overseas connections have now been dropped. But we do still take two children from Hong Kong and two from Bahrain.

Sydney

One of the Qantas staff at Sydney Airport who was responsible for the BA Crews when we were in Sydney has a daughter who was going through leukemia back in 1994. We decided to offer Allison a place on Dreamflight and her father, Derek Gascoine brought her over from Sydney to London. He did ask if he could come on the trip, but we explained that no parents went on the trip and we couldn't break our rule in this case either. Derek was very understanding and went off on a golfing trip from the UK whilst we were away.

Allison Porter (nee Gascoigne) came on Dreamflight in 1994. She has subsquently married and had two children. She is still in contact with me today and here is what she wrote for our newsletter in 2006. Thank you Allison for writing your story for us.

"In 1994 I had the pleasure of attending Dreamflight after being nominated by a close friend who worked for British Airways. I accepted the offer and had the most wonderful week of my life, meeting new people and making lifelong friends.

Since Dreamflight my life has changed (all positives). After graduating from school I was offered a job in the hospitality industry where I met a wonderful man named David (who later became my husband). I then studied to become a child care worker and worked in the industry for five years, before needing a change and now work as an accounts clerk for a national building supplies company.

In October 2002 I married David, did some traveling to Thailand, and the United Kingdom before building our dream home and having our first child, a beautiful baby girl, Isabelle Hope born on August 6th 2005.

My journey through treatment was very depressing and terrifying as I was old enough to realize what was happening to me, but with the help of family and friends I kept my chin up and NEVER GAVE UP.

I have written this letter to show parents and children who have gone through and are going through terrible times that there is light at the end of the tunnel, and that they should never give up, but most of all BELIEVE IN THEMSELVES and be confident.

Achievements of Dreamflight Children

The Paralympians

On Monday 15th September 2008 several members of the Dreamflight crew took to the skies and headed for Beijing on a work trip like no other. The crew were to bring home the British Paralympic team. They were invited to attend the closing ceremony at the "Birdsnest Stadium." Bless their hearts, the crew were phoning me from inside the Stadium to tell me all about it.

The paralympic team consisted of 206 athletes across 18 of the 20 events. On board the aircraft they not only had the team and support team but they had all the 102 medals including 42 golds, 29 silver, and 31 bronze.

During the flight two of the athletes recognised their crew member and said to them "you took me on Dreamflight as a child." Word went round the aircraft and another 5 athletes went into the galleys and said "we were on Dreamflight as well." Amongst them was Nyree Lewis who had been on the first Dreamflight in 1987. Dave Roberts who came in 1994 won four gold medals, Liz Johnson who went in 1997 (now a Dreamflight Patron), Kate Arnold who went in 2000, and David Smith who went in 2003.

above: Liz Johnson with Patricia and crew member Gillian Lloyd-Davies who had looked after Liz on her Dreamflight trip.

That September day for me personally was a very special day as the Dreamflight cabin crew were on the aircraft bringing them all home and I was fortunate enough to be asked by British Airways to be in the special "Meet & Greet" lounge with all the Olympians' families and friends awaiting their arrival home.

Dave Roberts came and put his four gold medals round my neck and said, "these are for you Pat for changing my life", I am so humbled by these wonderful athletes and I am so proud of them.

Other Achievements

KAREN QUA (nee Wooley)

Karen was diagnosed with lymphoblastic leukaemia just before her 16th birthday. Karen had to undergo painful chemotherapy and radiotherapy treatments. In November 1988 she was given a place on Dreamflight due to someone dropping out at the last minute.

Karen came back on Dreamflight in 1991 as an escort looking after two Dreamflight children. In the meantime she secured a job with British Airways and every November right up to the present day Karen is always in the hangar to wave us off. She has been a fantastic supporter.

RUTH MCGOWAN

In 1989 Ruth McGowan came on Dreamflight as a child in the Flintstones Group.

Ruth has now written:

Having been in remission from leukaemia for four years I felt like a fraud. Nevertheless it was hard to decline the offer of what would be a holiday of a lifetime.

From the moment we left Glasgow it was fun, fun, fun! The days flashed by at the speed of the The Hulk at Islands of Adventure and the events followed effortlessly from one to another without a hitch.

In 2004 Ruth returned to Dreamflight in the capacity of doctor, and this is what she has written.

It has been a wonderful experience to be part of Dreamflight again, this time as the Flintstones Doctor. The differences from my teenage Dreamflight experience were dramatic. I was oblivious to all the organisation that takes place; the meetings, discussions about the children, and that the "Library" was not used for finishing the holiday novel at the end of the day!

However, the whirl of Space Mountain, the soaking of Splash Mountain, and the sunny day at Blizzard Beach brought memories flooding back of how special those events were for me in 1989. This time I've enjoyed the magic of sharing this with the young Flintstones and that has meant more to me than anything. I'm uncertain which Dreamflight experience has moved me more.

JEFF DORMER

In 1997 after a serious illness Jeff joined us on his "holiday of a lifetime." In 2004 Jeff joined us again this time as an escort.

These were Jeff's comments after completing the trip as an escort:

The main difference between the trips was obviously "hard work". As a child I was unaware what went on behind the scenes to keep the Dreamflight machine well oiled and running smoothly. Despite all the hard work it was a real privelege to be involved in Dreamflight for a second time.

I consider myself lucky to have experienced Dreamflight from both perspectives.

Jeff has been back with us as an escort for a further two years. Thank you Jeff.

Muriel Searl who was Jeff's group leader of the Flintstones group wrote this when Jeff came back as an escort. "When I saw Jeff appear with his ORIGINAL white rucksack from 1997 I just couldn't believe my eyes! He had kept it for 7 years, with all his souvenirs inside, and dusted it down for his new role. It's not just for 10 days is it? It can change lives so much"

15. Patrons and Celebrities

• •

With the start of Dreamflight we decided we needed a couple of patrons who were well known. We first approached Sir Colin Marhsall as he was then (now Lord Marshall) to become President and he kindly agreed.

We then approached Bobby Moore and Jimmy Tarbuck. In 1999 Sir Cliff Richard OBE became a patron and more latterly they have been joined by Charlie Dimmock, Ian Poulter, and Liz Johnson.

Bobby Moore OBE

My dear friend Stephanie was married to the all time great footballer Bobby Moore. I phoned her and asked to speak to Bobby to see if he would do us the honour of becoming a patron. Imagine my complete

left: Bobby with Helly Copeland on the first trip in 1987

surprise when he said, "no-one will know of me Pat". My reply was "don't worry Bobby, we will put a name badge on you." Can you imagine the great Bobby Moore thinking that no-one would know him! The man who had captained England to win the World Cup in 1966 against Germany.

Bobby was a fantastic supporter. He would turn up to the smallest fete in Hayes and to a hotel at Heathrow where someone was doing a 24 hour swim, nothing was too much trouble for him.

Bobby also came with Stephanie to see Dreamflight off on several occasions. The children loved to meet him and get his autograph. I was devastated when I heard about his cancer, it shouldn't have happened to such a wonderful man. I can remember him ringing me after I had had an operation to check how I was. He was so thoughtful. Please see a section on Bobby in the fundraising section of this book.

I was invited to attend Bobby's memorial service at Westminster Abbey on Monday 28th June 1993. A very sad day but a wonderful tribute to him and a celebration of his life.

Jimmy Tarbuck OBE

We were very pleased when Jimmy Tarbuck accepted our offer to be a patron. He and Bobby Moore were great friends. Jimmy being the great golfer that he is has attended golf days that have been run for Dreamflight. Along with his lovely wife Pauline, who is also a keen golfer.

Lotus Supertravel run a Dreamflight Golf Tournament in the Algarve every January and Jimmy comes along and plays on one of the days and then attends the Gala Dinner in the evening.

Jimmy and I were featured in an article in Portugal's Algarve Magazine.

Sir Cliff Richard CBE

In 2009 we celebrated Sir Cliff being a patron for ten years. Cliff is a very active patron and attends as many departures of the flight as he can. He has also held three fundraising balls at Wentworth raising incredible amounts of money. Cliff and I attended a carol concert at

above: Pat with Jimmy in the Algarve

left: Sir Cliff with Patricia in the hangar ready for departure.

90

Eton, the money being donated to Dreamflight. That was another wonderful evening.

Charlie Dimmock

A few years back I had the pleasure of being on the crew that took Charlie Dimmock from London to New York. The upshot of all this was I managed to talk Charlie in to becoming a Dreamflight supporter. Well, she has gone further than that. To date Charlie has accompanied us on seven trips to Orlando and is allocated two children to look after for the 10 days. Charlie puts her heart and sole into giving the children a fantastic time. She really is a hard worker and we love having her on the trips with us. Two years ago we asked Charlie to become a Patron and of course we are delighted that she accepted.

I thought you might like to read this article written for a newsletter:

Who do you have to be to avoid US Customs, obtrusive fingerprint scanning, and waiting in an overcrowded departure lounge?

Who gets their own aircraft, handpicked crew, and stellar service and care?

Who receives a police motorcade to and from the airport?

The US President? The Pope? No, believe it or not it's Charlie Dimmock on her Dreamflight trips!

above: Ian with Patrica, Shaun, Emily and Aidan, three past Dreamflight children who all play golf and were in Pat's team "The Dreamflight Wonders"

Ian Poulter

Through Ian's caddie, Terry Mundy, Ian has become involved with Dreamflight and is such a great supporter. Not only does he donate articles for auctions at our various golf days, but nominated Dreamflight to benefit from the Tavistock Cup event held in March 2009. It is when Ians' club (Lake Nona) plays Tiger Woods' club (Isleworth) in Orlando. It's a fantastic event and Ian gave me a ticket to attend. You cannot buy tickets for this event as it is by invitation only. You have to wear the colours of the club you are supporting and there are no ropes to stay behind like in normal events, but you can walk down the fairways with the players. You just see this sea of blue (for Lake Nona) and red for (Isleworth) surging down the fairways. I have attended on three occasions now and in March 2011 there were four teams. Lake Nona, Isleworth, Albany in the Bahamas, and Queenwood. All four complexes are owned by the Tavistock Group.

When Ian married Katie, Ian phoned up and said "we have been together for 12 years, we have two children, we have all the pots and pans that we need so we have decided to have donations to charity instead of wedding presents". Ian split the donations between ourselves and the Willow Foundation which is run by the footballer Bob Wilson and his wife. Bob I had met through Bobby Moore. I was invited to the evening celebrations of the wedding at Woburn Abbey.

In 2009 Ian very kindly accepted our offer to become a patron. He and his lovely wife were on the tarmac to great us when we landed at Orlando Airport. The Golf Channel had come along to film all of this. On the trip over I had discovered that two of our young Dreamflighters played golf. Aidan Healey played off a handicap of 25 and Damien played off of 12. Ian escorted both of these youngsters down the aircraft steps. A big thrill for them to meet one of their golfing idols. The Golf Channel decided that Dreamflight was much bigger than they had imagined and wanted to film more of the charity. They worked very closely with our own video team and swapped footage both ways. They came down in the middle of the week and set up a "studio" to do interviews with myself, John Tye, Dr Simon Bailey, etc., and of course Ian who had come to the hotel with his own children to enjoy our "Hawaiian Evening." They were also there to film our departure at the end of the trip. Can you also imagine my surprise to discover that the freelance cameraman they had hired had actually been a Dreamflight video cameraman in years past and had married a daughter of one of our American escorts and had moved to the United States. It was lovely to have Greg there. Thank you the Golf Channel, I really appreciated how you showed the charity, and thank you Ian for putting it on your webpage and also on your twitter page.

In 2010 we ran our first Ian Poulter Dreamflight Golf Day at Woburn, his home Club in England. It was fantastic having Ian and his family with us and turned out to be a great fundraiser. This is now going to be repeated on a yearly basis. Ian also surprised us that evening by making a very large donation he had received from playing in a corporate charity day.

We ran the event again in July 2011 and another past Dreamflight child, Damien Hewitt played.

It is wonderful to have these children come and play in such a great fundraising event for the charity.

I wonder if I will find more young golfers on future trips!

Liz Johnson

Liz came on Dreamflight in 1997. In 2008 she went to Beijing as part of the Paralympic Swimming Team. On the flight back to the UK she recognised one of the cabin crew as someone who had taken her on the Dreamflight trip. Liz won a gold medal at Beijing and has now become one of our patrons. In 2011 she came back on the trip but this time as an adult. We are so proud of her.

right: Liz with her gold medal from Beijing.

Laura Davies, Johanna and Samantha Head

From the Ladies' Professional Golf Tour we have been supported so much by Laura Davies, Johanna Head (now married to Terry Mundy, Ian Poulters caddie), and Johanna's twin sister Samantha. How I treasure their friendships. All of them donate items to be auctioned and allow us to auction themselves for people to have a round of golf with them. Johanna, Terry, and Samantha have also been to meet the children both in London and in Orlando.

Jill Dando

Jill Dando, the television presenter, and a great friend of Sir Cliff, came to a couple of our departures prior to her untimely death. What a lovely lady she was. Her memorial service was at All Souls Church, Langham Place in London on 28th September 1999. I was invited to the service and what a very sad occasion it was.

Gloria Hunniford

Gloria is another great friend of Sir Cliff who has come along with him to the departure and the Fundraising Balls. I can remember on the departure of one flight, as we were taxiing out' we suddenly had three police motorbikes alongside. On the back of each motorbike were Gloria Hunniford, Faith Brown, and Jill Dando.

Roy Castle

Roy Castle was involved in the very first Dreamflight as the BBC came and did a live broadcast from the hotel as the children were checking in. They had originally asked if we could go to the studios. After we had explained that there was no way we could leave the hotel that morning the powers that be decided to come to us. It was great sitting on the sofa with Roy asking us and the children questions. He was really great at putting you at ease.

Rolf Harris and Jeremy Beadle

In the early years Rolf Harris and Jeremy Beadle would come along to the pre-trip party and entertain the children.

The Cast of the Bill

Over the last few years quite a few of the cast of The Bill have been coming along to the party to chat to the children and sign autographs. As the years have gone on more and more of the cast have turned up. In January 2009 Andrew Lancell and Gary Lucy were on Celebrity Millionaire and raised £25,000 for us.

Gordon Kaye and Carmen Silvera

They were always popular with the children especially those that had watched Allo, Allo.

Ant and Dec

Ant and Dec (Anthony McPartlin and Declan Donnelly) came to see the flight off in 2006. They were very impressed and I later met them down in Portugal on a golfing trip.

Patsy Palmer

Patsy is the cousin of one of the Dreamflight crew members and she persuaded Patsy to come and join in at the party and the departure in 2008. Bless her, she was moved to tears by the children. Patsy is well known for playing Bianca in Eastenders.

Chico – Yousseph Slimani

Chico came to fame for being on the X Factor and his "Chico Time." He has been involved for several years now and is so enthusiastic and the kids just love him.

Shane Ritchie

Actor, comedian, television presenter, singer, media personality, and well known for his part in East Enders.

Shane is a great supporter of Dreamflight and has been along on several occasions to wave the childen off on their long flight to Orlando.

Paul Barber

Paul Barber has been a stanch supporter of Dreamflight over many years and is always at the party the night before our departure and is in the hangar to wave us off.

16. Fundraising Events

It always amazes me the variety of fundraising events that have taken place over the years. Here is a summary of just a few of them. It is impossible for me to list them all, so I apologise to people whose events or efforts are not mentioned here.

Fundraising Gala Balls

The very first event was a ball run by myself at Great Fosters Hotel in Egham. It was the night we announced that the next morning we had a meeting with Sir Colin Marshall (as he was then – later to become Lord Marshall) to tell him about this wild idea called Dreamflight. We asked all our friends to support us if we managed to get the project off the ground. As you now know it become a reality.

A ball has been held every year since. It has grown over the years and we have had to move venues in order to accommodate everyone. We first moved to the Exclesior Hotel at Heathrow and then the Marriott Hotel, the Beaumont Conference Centre near Windsor, and now we have moved to the Hilton near Terminal 5, Heathrow. My dear friend Gillian Conway took over the running of the ball for a while, then Carol Garland and now it is run by Gillian Lloyd-Davies, Neil & Claire Parsons, Kelly & Jamie Keating, and Phil Ticehurst. There have been various themes for the evenings including The Blackberry Ball, Snowball, Bond Ball, Crystal Ball, Havana Ball, Hollywood Ball, Masquerade Ball, Advent Ball, Best of British, and the Roaring Twenties to name a few. Nowadays this is our biggest single fundraising event of the year. Last year £117,000 was raised on the night.

left: Bobby Moore and Franz Beckenbauer the German Captain of the 1966 World Cup Team and myself.

Dinner and Football Weekend – Bobby Moore

Having Bobby as our patron was wonderful. He said he didn't want to just be a figurehead but wanted to be hands on.

He organised a whole weekend starting with a dinner/dance at the Watford Hilton in September 1989. The following morning Bobby had organised a football match. Bobby had flown over Franz Beckanbauer from Germany to play in his team. When you think that he was captain of the England team which beat Franzs' German team in the World Cup 1966 it was a wonderful thing to see. The two had become firm friends.

Also playing were Georgie Best, Graeme Souness, Alan Ball, and Pat Jennings. The managers of the two teams were Lawrie McMenemy and Malcolm Allison. As the teams came out on to the pitch, for a joke, Georgie Best was carried out on a stretcher to start the game. It was a wonderful weekend.

Wentworth Balls – Sir Cliff Richard

Sir Cliff Richard has also been on the committee for three Balls that have been held at Wentworth Golf Club. Also on the committee were Robin Williams, Gillian Conway (Pooh Bear group leader), and Jacqui Loveridge one of the Dreamflight cabin crew.

The Pink Ball was in 2008. It was attended by Sir Cliff, our Patron, and Gloria Hunniford, with guest stars Bobby Davro and Christopher Biggins. The honoured guests and absolute scene stealers of the night were four former Dreamflight children from Gillian's Pooh Bear group. They emerged to huge applause to be interviewed by Gloria about their Dreamflight experiences and favourite memories. They all spoke of the new self-confidence that they came home with. Then young Laura (a Dreamflight child) had written her own very special version of Cliff's song "Summer Holiday" which she agreed to perform and was joined on stage by Sir Cliff. Laura had renamed the song "Dreamflight Holiday." Not a dry eye in the house!

The Tigger Ball in Newcastle

For a number of years now the group from the Northeast of England which is the Tigger Group have run a ball in May. This is another fabulous event and a big fundraiser every year organised by Dr. James Hayden and Catherine Foster and their team of helpers.

Another cabin crew member Angela Quaglia organises a Ball on a smaller scale in the South but still a very successful evening.

The London Eye and Dinner/Dance
Cruising Down the Thames

On a perfect summers' evening in July 2002 Dreamflight supporters gathered at the foot of the London Eye "dressed to the nines" in all their finery for a "champagne flight" on the London Eye. This was followed by a sail on the Silver Sturgeon down the Thames to enjoy an evening of food and wine, entertainment, and fundraising. This event was repeated in the summer of 2003.

Dream Dinner

In October 2003 London's Langham Hilton was the scene for the Dream Dinner. This was arranged by the British Airways Culinary Council. Although the format was simple the results were stunning. The 5 top chefs of the council – all of whom held at least 1 Michelin star – would each prepare a dish and the meal would be accompanied by the very finest wines. The planning was undertaken by the council member, Nicholas Lander, the Food Correspondent for the Financial Times, and his wife TVs' Jancis Robinson. Michel Roux from the Waterside Inn at Bray, Vineet Bahtia, and Mark Edwards from Nobu were among the seven top chefs.

Tickets for this event were £500 a head and the evening raised £100,000. Thanks go to Mike Street who was then British Airways Head of Operations and Customer Service. Mike is still a great supporter of the charity.

24 Hour Swim

One of the first fundraising events was a 24 hour swim in the hotel pool at the Heathrow Penta (now named the Heathrow Renaissance). We all turned up at various times to support Alan. Bobby Moore arrived to greet Alan as he got out of the pool at the end of the 24 hours.

New Years' Day Swim

For many years now a group of foolhardy people from the Surrey area (called the Brass Monkeys) have braved the cold weather at Bournemouth to do a New Years' Day swim. One year even one of the past Dreamflight children joined them. Carol Whapshare, the group leader for this area was heavily involved in this.

Air Show

We had a Dreamflight Air Show at Cranfield in Bedfordshire on 20th September 1992. It was to be the last flight of one of the Vulcan bombers and we put a Dreamflight sticker on its bomb doors. We had a fly past by the Red Arrows and Alex Hall one of our group leaders did a wing walk. Great fun and a lovely day. It is estimated that 30,000 people attended the show.

Support from the Armed Forces and the Tornado Display Team

The Tornado F3 Display team with Flt Lt Richard "Dicko" Moyes, husband of Hannah Shore one of our doctors, was on the display team taking the Tornado all over Europe showing off its abilities and wowing the crowds at air shows. They decided that they would raise some money for charity. Over the course of the season with Flt Lt Gareth (Gaz) Littlechild they completed 71 displays over 19 weekends at over 40 venues in 7 countries to over 5 million people and in the process raised over £6,000 for their chosen charities. In October 2005 I flew to RAF Leuchars – the most northerly fighter station in Fife – to meet Dicko and Gaz and be presented with a cheque.

The Merlin Helicopter Team

During 2006 members of "Team Merlin" the display team from 28 (Army Cooperation) Squadron, based at RAF Benson in Oxfordshire, participated in a variety of airshows and events throughout the UK and overseas.

During these events they were fundraising and thankfully Dreamflight was the recipient of their fundraising activities. Gareth Attridge was the instigator of all this and I think it was because his girlfriend at the time (now his wife) was a member of the Dreamflight cabin crew.

Car Boot Sales

The very first car boot sale was a car boot sale with a difference. We took a British Airways bus to the boot sale in Ascot, plus we were allowed to sell off some of the old crockery and dishes that had been used on board.

Gala Night at Stringfellows

On the 14th June 1992 we held a televised celebrity gala evening at Peter Stringfellows Club in London. Another very interesting evening. Peter Stringfellow was very supportive. We also had the regimental band of the Royal Welsh march right through the club complete with their mascot the goat (and he is partial to a little drink of beer)! This was also the night we launched our new logo.

I think this was probably the first time that Stringfellows Night Club had ever had a full regimental band playing there. Of course, the band members thoroughly enjoyed themselves.

Parachute Jumps

Quite a few people have done parachute jumps and free fall jumps over the years. In the first year a group of people were jumping with the Red Devils Parachute Team at Aldershot. I really can't find any reason to jump out of a perfectly serviceable aeroplane! I did go up on one of the flights and watched them jump out from the first officers' seat. The captain, Micky Munn, then started to throw this little aeroplane around after the last parachutist had left the aircraft. I hated it and pleaded with him to get back on the ground. I really do prefer a big Jumbo around me that wallows its way around the world.

Back in 2000 Suzanne Bailey said her husband (who is Dreamflight's Medical Director) won't be joining her on a parachute jump as "he doesn't like heights."

Book Sales

Book sales are a great way of raising money. We started these off in the Flight Crew Report Centre. We still have one every month in the British Airways headquarters at Waterside thanks to Amanda McCarthy.

Marathons

There are now many running events around the country from full marathons to half marathons and other distances. Since the advent of webpages, etc. there is a great site called justgiving.com and people can register a page for their event and encourage donations on line. Absolutely brilliant and we get the tax back.

Not only have they been run in this country but in various venues around the world. My dear friend Maddy Field, not content with completing the London Marathon for us, flew out to Sydney to run in that marathon as well.

Our Tigger Group Leader, Catherine Foster (whose father is the runner Brendon Foster) ran the London marathon in 2007.

Ambers of Amersham Fashion Shows

There is a beautiful shop in Amersham in Buckinghamshire which is housed in a 15th century mill. Lovely fashions, hair and beauty, and coffee shop. The very first year the sister of the owner Alistair Cameron rode her horse from Amersham to Heathrow to raise money. Lindy, at that time, worked at Heathrow. Over the years Alistair has chosen Dreamflight as their charity at his fashion shows. Really lovely events and if ever you are near Amersham do pop in to the shop. Even for just a coffee where the mill stream runs through.

The Great Escape

Another great way of raising money was devised by a couple of our Dreamflighters who just happened to be in The Police Force. So guess what. The great escape was organised from the cells at Bedford Police Station. The idea is everyone has to break out of the prison and get as far as they can in 24 hours with no money! You then have to ring back and say where you are.

On the first "escape" that Alex Hall and Glenn Clements attempted, they managed to reach Los Angeles. For their second attempt Alex and Glenn had organised a helicopter to take them to Heathrow Airport and we had organised tickets on British Airways to Hong Kong where they were met by the Hong Kong Police Force.

I took this picture of them in the cells just prior to their "escape"

BT Round the World Yacht Challenge

One of the British Airways 747 captains, who had himself suffered with cancer and got through all of his chemotherapy treatments applied, and was accepted, to sail on the yacht that had a disabled crew crewing it on the BT Round the World Yacht race in 1996. Mike Austin decided he would get sponsorship for Dreamflight during the race. The yacht was called Time and Tide. When Mike reached Sydney he was having trouble with his hands and was flown back to the UK to seek treatment. The specialists in London decided that if he went back to the yacht with the continual strain on his hands at the helm, he would do permanent damage and would then not be able to handle a B747 on his return to work. Mike reluctantly had to give up the yacht challenge. However, he did request to fly to Capetown to wave them off on their sector from Capetown to Boston. Mike, myself, and about 10 other Dreamflight cabin crew set off on this journey. We had Prince Michael of Kent on board to be part of the departure ceremony as well.

We went down to the harbour to have promotional photos taken before they left. Can you imagine how that yacht crew must have felt. There they were, trying to prepare for the long sector from Cape Town to Boston, and there was this British Airways crew clambering all over their yacht just to have photos taken. They then had to go out to do a couple of hours sailing trails and on their return they did invite us to join them for dinner and what fun we had with them.

The next morning we again went to the harbour for the departure ceremony. Bishop Desmond Tuto gave the blessing of the boats and made a special mention of the "Time and Tide crew." Mike and I had been invited onto the BBC launch to go out for the start of the actual race when the gun was set off. The rest of the crew had tried to hire a couple of small boats to come out as well, but as you can probably imagine there was not a boat to be had. Not to be put off, the rest of the flight crew had managed to charter a couple of small aircraft and flew out over the start as well. All good fun.

The next day on our flight home, Mike and I knew that we had quite a few family members of the yacht crews on board. I made an announcement asking for those that had relatives on a yacht to write down the name of the yacht, their name, and their family members names. I collected these and collated them in to the yacht names. One by one I took them to the flight deck and captain Mike managed to call the yacht and they could chat to their relatives. This took nearly two and a half hours to complete and we had Prince Michael on board again and he was the last one to send a message to all of the yacht crews. Well, that two and a half hours got me out of doing the normal meal service!

Mountain Climbs
In September 2004 cabin crew member Andrea O'Neill, together with 3 friends, climbed Mount Kilamanjaro in Africa. They had to battle biting cold winds, tiredness, steep ascents, and lack of oxygen. She said, "We had to stop gossiping as we couldn't breathe at an altitude of 20,000 feet."

Dr Richard Breene has recently climbed Mt Kilamanjaro.

Mount Fuji in Japan Climb
Neil Smith, one of the Dreamflight cabin crew, decided in 2009 to organise a team to climb Mt Fuji. Neil managed to get a crew together who would make the climb in their time off in Tokyo on a normal rostered trip. Quite a few ground staff and one of our group leaders, Catherine Foster, tagged along as well making a total of 34 intrepid climbers.

Neil subsequently organised the trip again in 2010 with the crew again climbing in their time off on a scheduled trip.

Three Peaks Challenge

In June 2004 a stalwart group led by Chris Homer did the three peaks challenge. That is to climb Ben Nevis, ScaFell Pike, and Snowdon in 24 hours. This effort was in memory of Justine Diaper, (A Mickey Mouse child in 2002) who inspired all who knew her by her great courage and wicked sense of fun. Her parents, Kevin – one of the climbers – and Beverley felt that Dreamflight was a big highlight in their daughter's life and wanted to commit to fundraising for the charity. Well done Mark Pizzey.

In July 2009 this journey was also undertaken by another group of Dreamflighters. Some of the Goofy Group (including the group leader Dr. Cathryn Chadwick) accompanied by some of the Simpsons Group and a contingent from Sterling Press.

Trekking the Inca Trail

In 2009 one of the Dreamflight cabin crew (Lynn Ball) and one of the nurses (Tricia McGinnity) decided to do the Inca Trail. They spent 4 days and 3 nights camping in the Andes. Very well done girls, I know you said it wasn't easy but you told me the inspiration to keep going was "the Dreamflight children."

Absails

There have been people who have been mad enough to absail from buildings.

In 2002 Debbie Beedie, a BA Sales and Marketing Manager for British Airways based in Bahrain, absailed down a 14 storey building in the UK accompanied by her 77 year old Mum!

Bowls

Jim and Daphne Parsons have been instrumental in getting some of the bowls clubs in raising money for Dreamflight over a number of years. Jim and Daphne, whose son Neil is on the Dreamflight cabin crew, also run our merchandising stall at the hotel when we depart.

Christmas Lights

In December 2003 about ten days before Christmas I was watching GMTV and they were showing different houses all decorated up for Christmas. They showed a house near Reading and announced they were raising money for Dreamflight.

I contacted GMTV and asked them to pass on my telephone number to the people concerned as I wanted to thank them. Gary from Reading phoned me and I couldn't believe it as I had known him for some 37 years. Gary was a flight engineer and we had flown together on numerous occasions.

I went over to see his house and he had over 35,000 little white lights. It was the first year he had collected for charity and not only that the village pub opposite, "The Swan", also adopted Dreamflight. To this day the landlord at "The Swan" is still a huge supporter and Dave Woodward has been on several Dreamflights as an escort.

Over a number of years various people have decorated the outsides of their houses and asked for donations for Dreamflight.

The Great Scottish Walk

David Smyth and friends have raised money over the years with "The Great Scottish Walk." A 12 mile walk around Edinburgh.

In 2007 Bruce Zweggat (one of our dedicated American escorts) flew over from Orlando to participate in this walk. He was joined by 15 other walkers from the Flintstones group and 3 little ducklings from the Donald Duck Group.

Long Cycle Rides

There have been quite a number of people who have cycled long rides in aid of Dreamflight and here I mention just a few.

In 2007 Guy Townsend and the Walker Hamill team broke the record for cycling across the French Pyrenees. The facts were daunting: 750 km, 21 mountain passes, 16,000 of ascent – equivalent to riding up Everest twice. The team were determined to smash the previous record of 4 days. Guess what, they set a new record of 3 days. On 27th June

2007 the team pedalled into Port Argelles, exhausted but happy having completed the ride in 60 hours.

London to Glasgow Bike Ride
On 22nd August 2009 Laura Shave, who is one of the Dreamflight escorts and works for British Airways, cycled from BA's Head Office at Heathrow Airport to Glasgow. She cycled up hill and down dale for 10 days.

John O'Groats to Lands End
In 2010 a dear friend of mine cycled the length of the UK for Dreamflight. Well done Jonathan McKay.

Schools
It is interesting that schools like to get involved with fundraising. Children love to help other children. They do all sorts of things including dress-down days. My own local school, The Gateway in Great Missenden raised over £3,000 which paid for one childs' holiday. They had a Summer Fun Day with a Victorian Theme. They had a Town Crier, Cream Teas, Fairground Rides, BBQ, various stalls, and a Childrens' assault course.

Day Trips in to Europe
I have made friends with a lovely chap called Chris Harrott through various golf days. Chris was a captain with Britannia Airways and was also heavily involved with a group of Rotarians from Bedford. On a couple of occasions they chartered an aircraft and arranged day trips into Europe. I went on one of them to Prague. It was great fun and I couldn't believe that all the Britannia Airways crew were behind us. Chris organised another one to Budapest and then I managed to go on the one to Venice. Chris has been a tireless fundraiser and still is, and I still enjoy a game of golf with him, and thank you to the Bedford Park Rotarians Club.

Zip Wire

More recently a fun way of fundraising seems to be participating in a zip wire. Several of our group leaders have organised for escorts and friends in their area to participate.

As I said at the beginning of this chapter, there are so many wonderful ideas that people have come up with to help fundraise for us. I would need a seperate book to list them all and, more importantly, to list the names of everyone involved. I really am so grateful to each and every single one of you and I am truly sorry that I cannot mention everyone's name. I do hope you will forgive me but understand why I can't list every event and every participant.

Fundraising Golfing Events

Right from the very beginning golf has featured heavily in our fundraising programme and that is not just because I enjoy playing golf myself!

The very first Dreamflight golf day was organised at the great Wentworth Golf Club in Sunningdale. Bobby Moore and Jimmy Tarbuck, being the patrons, came and played along with Jimmy's wife Pauline and other celebrities like Henry Cooper. It was a huge success. One of the participants of the day was the manager of the Moor Park Golf Club. He made us an offer that night, that if we took the Tournament to his Club the next year he would donate all the tee times. To this day this still happens and our Tournament there is in April. Over the years thousands of pounds have been raised.

The second golf fundraising day was a small event at Chiltern Forest Golf Club in Buckinghamshire. I was a member there at the time.

The golf club that I am a member of now is Mentmore Golf and Country Club near Leighton Buzzard. We have been chosen as the Lady Captain's charity twice before when Ann Latham and Pat Bannister were the captains. Last year 2010/11 both the Mens' and the Ladys' Captains at Mentmore chose us for our 25th year. Thank you Carolyn McKewan and Jon Dymock.

Muriel Searl, our Flintstones Group Leader organised a golf day in Scotland and Cathryn Chadwick (our Goofy Group Leader) now organises a yearly golf day at Overstone Park in Northampton.

One of the ground staff members at BA used to organise a golfing holiday in the United States. One particular year it was organised at Fort Lauderdale and Peter Cook and Kenny Lynch went over to play in it. I organised to operate a flight out to Florida and I drove straight up to Fort Lauderdale to do the after dinner speech. I then operated the flight home the next day with Peter and Kenny and most of the golfers on board.

In 2008 the captain of Wentworth Golf Club, Neil Mutton, chose Dreamflight as his captain's charity and raised in excess of £100,000.

BACC Golf Day in Orlando

On the other side of the Atlantic we also have a fundraising golf day. The original one was organised by the manager of the Holiday Inn hotel where we stay. His name is Lenny Stark and he was a New Yorker and brought up in the Bronx. He used to frighten me to death when I went to his office to negotiate the contract for the hotel each year. On one occasion we had decided to stay on for a few days vacation at the end of all the negotiations. We had decided to play golf and were walking through the hotel lobby with our golf clubs when Lenny spotted us. He said he had no idea that we were golfers and that he would arrange for us to play at one of the Disney courses. It was a great day and we all ended up having lunch afterwards and plenty of chatting. That was when Lenny discovered that Dreamflight was not organised, or more importantly, not paid for by British Airways. He then stated that, in that case, he had better start raising money to pay for the hotel bill at his own hotel! The day is now organised by the British American Chamber of Commerce in Orlando and for most years I do manage to organise my trip to Orlando to do the negotiations and contracts for the trip around the time of the golf day so that I can be there to support it.

In 2009 they telephoned me to say that they had a new fundraising idea to start the day off. Everyone would be asked to buy golf balls with numbers on them. Just prior to the tee off time, a helicopter would take off and the balls would be dropped on to one of the greens. The ball nearest the hole would give the winner $1,000. What they failed to tell me was that I was the one to go up in the helicopter to drop the balls. The only helicopter ride I had done previously to this was in New York and I absolutely hated it. When I get airborne I like to have a big 747 aircraft around me. The things you have to do in the name of charity! At the appointed time I arrived to get in the helicopter only to discover that they had taken the door off to make it easier for me to tip this bucket of balls out. I have to say, it wasn't as bad as I thought it was going to be. I wasn't quite shaking to bits when we came down and I then had to tee off.

Fanny Sunnesson

Fanny Sunnesson who now caddies for Henrik Stenson was caddying for Nick Faldo when I first met her. I met her on a flight from Los Angeles to London. I became friendly with her and she has supported us by obtaining items for us to auction and in one copy of Golf World magazine did a caricature of herself which raised money for us. Fanny also gave me tickets to attend the Ryder Cup at the Belfry in 1993.

Johanna and Samantha Head and Terry Mundy Golf Day

Johanna, Samantha, and Johanna's then boyfriend (now her husband) organised a fundraising golf day at the Bedford Golf Club in December 2003. All three are totally dedicated to Dreamflight. The day finished at their local pub and raised £10,000.

It was Terry who persuaded Ian Poulter to get involved, so I owe a huge debt to Terry. Thank you most sincerely Terry.

Dan Jaffe Golf Day in France

Dan Jaffe who had been our Dreamflight first officer for ten years lives in Mougin near Nice in the South of France. He decided he wanted to do a fundraising golf day for us and quite a team of us flew down for a couple of days. It was held at the Royal Mougin Golf Club on September 10th 2005. 71 golfers participated and the evening party had 170 guests with live jazz, piano, and a champagne reception. Dan was always in the Pluto Group which was from Wales. One year he had become particularly friendly with one of the Welsh boys and they kept in regular contact. He spoke to the parents and it was agreed that Dan would fly him and his parents to be at the golf day. Dan had asked him to write a speech for Dan to read out at the dinner saying what Dreamflight meant to him. On the day, his parents had told him he was flying to Paris to visit Euro Disney. Can you imagine his surprise when he came through Nice Airport Terminal and he was not in Paris but in Nice and Dan was waiting to pick them up. Dan said to him "now you can read your own speech out". It was a very emotional evening.

Helen and Maddy's Golf Days

Two very good friends of mine from my flying days have both been escorts on the trip. Maddy Field and Helen Taylor have arranged a couple of fundraising golf days at Henley Golf Club.

As we approach our 25th Anniversary in 2011 there are quite a few more golf events going on. We have been chosen by the following captains as their charity.

Bucks County, Ladys Captains' charity
Lambourne, Mens Captains' charity
Ferndown, Bournemouth, Ladys Captains' charity
Grims Dyke Golf Club near Harrow, Mens Captains' charity
Oaklands Park, Chalfont St Peter, Ladys Captains' charity

The Goofy Golf Days

In 2006 the Goofy Group organised a golf day which has now become an annual event. In 2008 they had severe storm warnings but still, 21 intrepid teams turned up and played. Unfortunately I was not able to make it that year but I have on another couple of occasions. Always a lovely day and thank you Cathryn Chadwick (Goofy Group Leader) and her team.

Corporate Sponsorships

Apart from British Airways who have always supported us we were approached a few years ago by the Spar Grocery stores as they wanted to adopt us as a charity. This was followed by a request from Autoglass and then Diners Club.

British Airways

As you'll have been able to tell by now, flying and British Airways run through my veins, so I guess it's not surprising that the charity I co-founded is intrinsically linked to British Airways. I am very proud to say that we have been supported by British Airways for 25 years. They have not only given us many flights over the years for fundraising, but they crucially enable us to make the flight itself part of an amazing experience for the children. The check-in from the comfort of our Heathrow hotel, the 'party' at the engineering base before we board the aircraft, the rostering of our own cabin crew and pilots – none of this could happen without British Airways and the many Dreamflight supporters at 'my favourite airline'. We do, however, pay for the charter of the aircraft.

Spar Grocers

In 1992 Spar were our very first major corporate sponsor. Bill Stratton who was the Marketing Services Controller accompanied us on the trip as an escort. Spar were to support us for two years and over that time they raised over £350,000 for us, mainly raised by their staff. They found it was a great way of the staff getting together in their own time and building friendships that then benefited their working relationships.

Autoglass

We were then approached by Autoglass to be their charity for two years. From this relationship one of their staff, Robert Bass who was Company Secretary, became very involved. Robert co-ordinated the fundraising activities and subsequently came on the trip as an escort for four years. In 2005 we were delighted to welcome Robert to the board of Dreamflight trustees.

On 16th May 1992 The Autoglass Trophy was played at Wembley between Stockport County and Stoke City. Prior to the main match there was a charity match in aid of Dreamflight. I attended the luncheon with Bobby Moore and just before the kick-off of the main match I was led up through the tunnel by Sir Stanley Matthews and on to the hallowed turf! If only my father had been alive to see this as he was passionate about his football and obviously was a great fan of Stanley Matthews. Once on the turf the Red Devils Parachute Team parachuted in with the ball for the match and handed it to me to pass on to start the match. The man who parachuted in with the ball had actually been on Dreamflight as an escort on the very first Dreamflight. I then sat in the Royal Box with Bobby Moore to watch the match.,

above: Sir Stanley Matthews, myself, and Robert Bass.

Today's pre-match entertainment organised by The Football League will involve a celebrity football match with stars from football and other sports.

© 1987 The Walt Disney Company

The two teams representing Stoke City and Stockport County will be playing on behalf of DREAMFLIGHT - a charity in aid of sick and disabled children.

The match itself will be 15 minutes each half with a well needed 5 minute half-time interval.

In the Stoke City side, will be well known ex-players Terry Conroy and Jimmy Greenhoff whilst Stockport County will be represented by prolific striker Les Bradd and loyal club servant John Rutter. Stoke will also be led out by Tony Waddington, Manager of the famous 1972 League Cup winning side.

The match will be refereed by Football League official Neil Midgeley and at the end of the match Sir Stanley Matthews CBE will present the Charity Cup to the winning side and receive a cheque on behalf of DREAMFLIGHT from the sponsors, Autoglass.

Due to the kind sponsorship of Autoglass an opportunity has also been given to several members of the general public to play in the match as well.

Get behind your team and give the players real encouragement so that they can raise their game enough to make Graham Taylor's European Championship squad!

Thank you!

WHAT IS DREAMFLIGHT?

DREAMFLIGHT is a registered UK charity whose purpose is to send incurably ill, sick or disabled children on their 'holiday of a lifetime' to Disneyworld in Florida.

While many charities devote their energies to funding long term research projects or the purchase of expensive medical equipment, DREAMFLIGHT thinks it is just as important to bring some fun and joy into the lives of children who perhaps can't wait long enough for the medical breakthrough they need. Other DREAMFLIGHT children are now quite healthy, but because of the suffering they endured during their illness, DREAMFLIGHT feels they deserve a holiday like this.

HOW WAS DREAMFLIGHT STARTED?

The original concept was devised in 1986 by a small group of British Airways staff and their considerable dedication and energies culminated in a Boeing 747 full of 288 sick children and their adult helpers, flying off to Disneyworld for five magical days in November 1987. The original DREAMFLIGHT was only intended to be a 'one off' trip but the '87 flight was such a success that it has now become an annual event.

If you would like further information about DREAMFLIGHT, or how you could help, please contact: Patricia Pearce & Derek Pereira, 4 Saxeways, Chartridge Lane, Chartridge, Bucks HP5 2SH. Telephone: (0494) 792991.

AUTOGLASS

CHARITY MATCH

Diners Club

Following on from the above two corporates we then had a two year association with Diners Club.

British Airways used to use Diners Club cards to pay the crew allowances down route. Richard Church, who was the interface between British Airways and Diners Club, very kindly talked to his counterpart in Diners Club to see if they would take up sponsorship of Dreamflight. This they very kindly did for two years.

17. BA Dreamflight – The Horse

I belong to a group of 20 people, most of whom are current or former BA staff. I am nearly two years old but am quite big for my age and incredibly handsome. My dad was a brilliant racehorse called Noverre. I will make my racing debut at Windsor. I hope you like my photograph looking at the banner of the charity I have been named after.

The consortium asked the staff members of British Airways in the BA News to name the horse. The winning name was BA Dreamflight.

When BA Dreamflight did his first race at Windsor I was invited along and went into the owners circle alongside the owners who included Martin Broughton (The Chairman of British Airways). I was interviewed on the Racing Channel. Well, those of you who know me, know that I know nothing about racehorses! When I was asked about his chances in the race all I could think to say was "well he is only a baby and it is his first race".

Within five minutes I had received 3 text messages from Dreamflighters saying they had seen me on the television. I never realised how many gamblers there were in Dreamflight!

On one occasion we took two Dreamflight children, who were mad keen on horses, down to meet BA Dreamflight at the stables. The trainer, Hughie Morrison, and stable girl Victoria were so amazed at how gentle and quiet the horse was when the children were with him. It was as if he knew.

He is now owned and cared for by Victoria Cartmel, the girl who used to look after him at the stables. Initially he had difficulty in getting used to just being a normal horse again, he had done a lot of racing and it took its toll, unfortunately this manifested itself physically as well as psychologically. In the very last stages of his racing career

left: " I am quite big for my age and incredibly handsome" (That is the horse saying that and not me.)

he picked up an injury to one of his rear legs and this flared up after his retirement, to the extent that a vet suggested to Victoria that she might consider having him put down. Naturally, Victoria and Robert Winston (Victoria's partner) would have none of that and they cared for the horse through a long (and expensive) recuperation period. I am pleased to say that he is now back to rude health and in a much calmer and happier state of mind. In his career he had one win, two second place finishes, and two third places.

Poor Victoria had to cope with all this while herself recuperating from an awful fall on the gallops in which she shattered her ankle – an injury which she is still feeling the effects of almost a year later.

Victoria and Robert are moving to a small yard of their own near Deauville in France at the end of February 2011 and her beloved 'Bee' will be going with her. The horse has been schooled over jumps with a view to entering him in show-jumping in ex-racehorse classes on this side of the channel, maybe this summer. Victoria has her eyes on

Windsor, Newbury, Stoneleigh, etc. Naturally, she knows just how important BA Dreamflight was/is to us all (and us to him).

Bob's Dreamflight

A very dear friend of mine Bob Stocker was a British Airways captain and he and his wife Mavis became great supporters of Dreamflight. He always used to take a table at our fundraising balls and always came to Portugal every January for the Dreamflight Golf Tournament. He also organised the Moor Park Golf day for us for a number of years.

Sadly Bob passed away in 2009 and his wife Mavis had donations to Dreamflight rather than flowers at his funeral. So generous of you Mavis.

Whilst I was at the funeral I met a gentleman who told me he was a horse trainer and a very good friend of Bob's, D K Ivory, and that he would like to name a horse "Dreamflight" in memory of Bob. I advised him that there was a horse called BA Dreamflight, so he decided there and then to call the horse "Bob's Dreamflight."

Bob's Dreamflight had 2 wins, 5 seconds and 2 third place finishes.

18. Dreamflight Flight and Cabin Crews

Over the years we have had quite a few cabin and flight crew members and some have been involved for many years.

I myself was the first Cabin Service Director but I went as supernumerary (extra crew), because I had so much on my mind with the organisation of the whole trip.

I had flown with cabin crew member Derek Stoddard quite a few times prior to the start of Dreamflight and I particularly remember one trip to Los Angeles. Derek knew of a little boy who had been diagnosed with a brain tumour. Derek had asked British Airways to donate tickets for the family of four so that they could enjoy a holiday together. Not only did British Airways donate the tickets but arranged for Derek to travel as supernumerary crew on the flight out, stay with them in Los Angles, and then operate the return flight. I was on the outbound sector. Little Robert Greaves (who was seven years old) was a delight to have on board. I had him working in the cabin with me in first class. The actor Robert Conrad was a passenger in the first class cabin, and asked what little Robert was doing. I explained about his illness and that he didn't have many weeks to live. Robert Conrad arranged for "little" Robert to visit 20th Century Fox and meet Lee Majors and generally helped to look after the Greaves family. Sadly little Robert lost his fight for life not many weeks later.

I was fortunate enough to meet Robert's parents at the very first fundraising event that Derek Stoddard organised in Portsmouth. At this event I will never forget coming out of the Ladies toilets during the evening and an older man came out of the Gents leaning on a stick. He said to me "I haven't got much money but I would like to make a donation". He placed a £1 coin in my hand. To this very day I can still feel that £1. Some people, and indeed, companies, can make big donations, but I have always remembered that the small amounts are so important as well. All those small amounts make a big amount at the end of the day.

I often think it was this event which made me realise that children with health problems do deserve a treat in life.

Derek Stoddard was always my right hand man from the very beginning and stayed on the crew until his retirement from Dreamflight and British Airways in 2004. I myself retired from British Airways six months later.

Thank you Derek for the wonderful years of friendship.

The Flight Crew

Our flight and cabin crew never cease to amaze me. Uniform regulations seem to go out of the window! In the past three years I have been so awsestruck and surprised at the lengths the flight crew go to with their "uniforms" I never know what they are going to turn up as.

2010 They were Gladiators

When we leave Orlando airport, the crew have to walk through the main passenger terminal to collect the aircraft and then taxii it over to the private jet terminal where we depart from. Without exception, every crew member says it is so funny walking through the Airport Terminal in their fancy dress. They have lots of children who are travelling on other airlines saying they want to fly with the Dreamflight airline.

The crew not only operate the flight but stay with us for the whole ten days. They are allocated to a group and work with that group for the duration of the trip.

A briefing for a normal British Airways flight takes about 10 minutes. The Dreamflight Briefing takes over an hour as it is not just about the flight but their duties during the holiday.

We have a crew roster for "pool" duties. Two or three crew will be rostered at 6 a.m each morning to act as a sort of lifeguard. When we arrive back from the theme parks the whole crew will be on duty at the pool. Not only that, on the first morning they have to blow up all the buoyancy aids that we have for the children.

above: In 2008 we had The Three Muskateers.

below: In 2009 they were World War II pilots

One year the captain obtained approval to fly over Disney. It is called a Disney arrival. Since the sad events of 9/11 this has not been allowed.

Another year the captain did a flypast at Cape Kennedy. We came down to 3,000 feet I think it was, and did what they call "a beat up of the runway" we then soared back up and away. Thanks captain, it made quite a few of the children sitting at the back of the aircraft quite airsick!

We have had many crew members over the years but having been cabin crew myself, my crews are always very special to me.

The BA Ground Staff

There are around 150 or so volunteers from BA ground staff and these are headed up by Paul Claro a Duty Terminal Manager. Paul has worked with us since the beginning. Paul has always said, "It is an honour and a privelege to play a small part in making Dreamflight the trip of a lifetime".

Paul also says, "Even now, it still amazes me how we can depart over 250 departures in a day seemingly without a hitch, let alone depart a flight from a hangar several miles from the main Terminal". Paul can always be picked out in the hangar by his loud voice giving instructions!

Darren Kennelly always manages to depart our aircraft on time.

above: This picture taken from the aircraft doorway looking down on all the ground helpers.

Steve Edwards from Aircraft Appearance ensures that Dreamflight is put on the side of the aircraft in big letters.

We have the baggage handlers who dress up in fancy dress just to load all our bags on the aircraft. The vehicles that lift the baggage containers and some 50 odd wheelchairs up to the aircraft holds only move at about 5 mph and they have to be brought from the Terminal. (some 7–8 miles away). This sort of equipment would not normally be needed at the British Airways engineering base.

The Engineers join in as well. They maintain the castle that they built for us back in 1987 and position it at the bottom of the steps ready for the children.

The catering staff load the aircraft and organise special menus to be printed.

Brummie somehow manages to conjure up BA coaches to transport us all from the hotel to the hangar, together with the Ground Transport Department.

Again, I do apologise that I have not managed to name everyone here. You know who you are and you know that I am very grateful for all the help and support you give.

19. Help and Support

The Video/Photography and Entertainment Teams

Still Photography

Our first photographer was a man named Alan Selwood. Alan was a member of British Airways ground staff and photography was his hobby. For many years Alan would race around the theme parks capturing all the children. Sometimes he would produce some 23 albums of the trip.

Our photographer now is John Cavanagh. John is a B777 pilot and guess what, photography is his hobby. Now it is John that is found racing around the theme parks instead of Alan. I think John is thankful that all the photography is now digital and not film as it was in Alans' day. John produces a DVD for each group to be put in a special commorative pack along with the video DVD.

Video and DVD

As mentioned in the earlier part of this book, the BBC came with us to make a documentary of the charity on the first trip. From this idea we decided that in following years we would take a video team to record the trip to be given to the parents. For several years we only made one video which covered all 192 children. The team made sure they somehow managed to catch each child, but sometimes if you blinked you would have missed them. Now we have a team of six or seven cameramen (who all volunteer their time) who cover two groups each. Each child will receive a DVD of approximately 90 minutes of just their group.

With valuable professional equipment the team shoot many hours of film.

The task when we arrive home from a trip for them is to get all those hours of recorded tape onto a computer and then the editing begins. This involves reviewing every recorded moment – and there could be up to 30 hours! – and deciding what to include in the final version. The sequences are cut and pasted using specialist editing equipment software. Music also has to be added along with the titles, credits, and other elements which make a video production. As one of the video team said, "It takes many many hours of work to turn 10 days of filming in to a 90 minute video but the result, and the memories make it all worthwhile."

Over the years their equipment has been changing and I gather that with digital now it is making it a lot easier. Instead of a video tape it is now DVDs.

These days, in "The Library" in the hotel in the evening you will see the video team with all their laptops on one table sharing footage, etc. between each other. I love to pop over and look over their shoulders.

I think it is really nice for the video team now that a number of group leaders organise a "premiere" of the video at their reunions at local cinemas and the camera person can see the reaction of the parents to seeing what their child managed to get up to!

I would like to mention here how sad it was that Leslie Tagaki, who came as a camera person and as an escort, sadly lost her battle with cancer. You are sadly missed Leslie.

The still photos and the DVDs are such an important part of Dreamflight and these days the teams are very involved in fundraising events during the year and not just the trip. It is great to have them around.

Entertainment Teams

Over the years we have had a few people involved in the entertainment side of the trip. One of the first to come on the trip was a clown called Trevor Pharo. Fay Presto and Mandy Muden (both top magicians) came for many years as well.

Tony Land ran the team for a while and now Jason Beamish-Knight is in charge.

Dreamflight on the Other Side of the Atlantic

We have always had a brilliant relationship with our volunteers on "the other side of the pond".

From the very first year the local people of Orlando have been helping and supporting Dreamflight. I am pleased to say that some have been with us from the very beginning. Others have joined along the way.

Americans are very much into their community helping and it was through the AT &T company that our first volunteers came from.

Now we have an American board set up consisting of six people. Each year they organise approximately 45 weekly American volunteers who check in to the hotel with us and are there for the duration of the trip. It is always a welcome sight to open the aircraft doors and stand at the top of the steps to see them waiting on the tarmac waving hands and donning their favourite character gear for their allotted group. They assist with unloading luggage, loading wheelchairs onto the buses and then accompany the groups to the hotel.

Along with the weekly helpers, they organise around another 20 or so daily volunteers who join us on a daily basis. We really do need all these pairs of hands.

On top of this they will organise the medical equipment we need to hire in including wheelchairs, lifting equipment, night feed pumps, etc. They also organise the hire of 40 radios and some cell phones to help with our communication.

Our board also fundraise in Florida. Every May they participate in Charity Challenge in Altamonte Springs. Teams take part to raise funds for many different charities. They have events like volley-ball, tug of war, obstacle course, basketball, canoe race, and a tube relay to name but a few. The highlight of the event is the Championship party held on the last evening when the prizes are awarded.

They also help out with the British American Chamber of Commerce who organise a charity golf day.

Debbie Zwegatt and her husband Bruce have been involved the longest. Others include Mitch Peavey, Steve Theibuth, Cindy Waldorf and her husband, Stephanie Sorantino, and Sandy Matusz (who used to be the British Airways manager at Orlando airport and now that she has retired she is on the Dreamflight USA board). Others who have helped over the years include Tommy and Dorothy Halliwell and John & Joane Elfring. Once again, my apologies that I haven't managed to list everyone.

A quote from one of our American helpers "Whether you have helped on Dreamflight for one year, 2 years or ever since 1987, one thing is for certain, you never forget the children that have touched your heart or the escorts that have become lifelong friends.

Nowadays I cannot believe the amount of adults that "cross the pond" either way, to stay with their Dreamflight friends.

This is taken from a letter from one of our wonderful American escorts that I thought you might like to read.

I am a scoutmaster for a troup in Florida. At the end of each meeting I try to say something meaningful to the scouts in what we call a scoutmaster's minute. The meeting after I had worked as a daily helper for Dreamflight, I shared my experience with the boys in my troop. What I was impressed with was their reaction. It went something like this:

"I want you all to do something for me. Without considering out loud, I want you to presume I am a magic genie that can grant you one wish. It can be anything you want, but you only get one, so make it a good one. Now hold that thought and listen to this. The other day I went and spent the day with a group of kids that had many different kinds of physical problems. A the end of the day something happened that made me think of things a bit differently. A park worker came over to us and asked if

we would like to help her feed the ducks. We followed her to the bridge and she passed out handfuls of food to give to the ducks waiting below. I was helping a young man with his wheelchair when he turned to me and asked me to help him throw the food. I stood there with a puzzled look till he explained that he wanted me to lift his arm and throw it forward. I did, he released the food, and then laughed at the way the ducks scrambled for it. We did this again and again, each time to his complete delight.

I wonder though ... if he were here tonight ... what his wish would be? Or, the boy who couldn't ride with us because the many pins in his spine could only hold him upright and wouldn't take the jostling of the truck ... what would he wish for? Or, the many kids there that day who were bald from going through agonizing treatments of chemotherapy ... what would their wish be?

Now think back to your wish. It looks different now, doesn't it? Does this mean that we shouldn't dream or wish for things anymore? Of course not, but sometimes ... at least tonight, try saying a prayer not asking for anything. Just say thank you for what you have, even it is only the ability to throw your own duck food.

The silence I had asked for at the start, continued for awhile when I finished, then they all started clapping. Something they had never done before. But, what really surprised me most was on the way home, my own son said, "Dad, that was the best scoutmaster minute you have ever done". It was then that I realised that, just maybe, this lesson got through to them.

I am sharing this story with you to let you know that your wonderful work in the Dreamflight programme doesn't stop with the kids you are caring for, but reaches out to many more including myself. And for that, I will always be grateful.

What a wonderful letter. It really made me realise how far reaching Dreamflight can be. It isn't always just about the trip.

Police Escorts and Fire Brigades

Both in the UK and in the USA we have great support from the police and fire brigades.

The Police

In the UK our police escort is provided by the Queens' 'Special Escort group' (SEG). What a fantastic bunch of guys these are. In fact, one of them came on the trip with us in 2010 as an escort and is returning again this year. They escort the buses from the hotel to the hangar. It is great to whizz through all the traffic lights with no stopping. The children, not to mention the adults, love this.

On two occasions now I have been invited to the SEG cocktail party in London. It is always a pleasure to meet the lads.

In the United States we are met by around 40 or more outriders. They circle round the aircraft when it comes to a stop on the tarmac with their lights flashing and their sirens blarring.

When we have loaded all 13 buses and are ready to depart from the aircraft to the hotel, they go ahead and close all the roads. They close the I4 which is like closing the M4 in the UK.

In 2010 I managed to get a lovely businessman in Orlando to lend us his helicopter so that we could put one of our cameramen on it to film an aerial view of our journey from the airport to the hotel. I love watching that short video.

Fire Brigades

On this side of the Atlantic several fire brigades have fundraised for us. The Amersham Fire Station lads walked from Aylesbury to Amersham with full kit on. They then brought their fire engine down to the hotel for the children to look at.

On taxiing out from the hangar, on occasions, the fire brigade have done an archway of water over the aircraft and the same happens when we arrive in Orlando. In Orlando also, as several firemen spend the week with us as weekly volunteers, they get their respective fire brigades to bring fire engines along.

Every year on the last day of the trip, the police and the fire brigade come and do a joint display in the hotel car park for the children. The police bring a helicopter, police cars, horses and dogs, etc. The fire brigade bring their fire engines for the children to clamber all over. There is so much noise in the car park that morning that I often wonder what people near the hotel think when they hear all these sirens going as the children press all the buttons.

In 2009 one of the children in the Donald Duck Group had his birthday on this particular day. He was going to go up on the firemans' ladder in the bucket but decided he would like me to go with him. Not liking heights but not wishing to disappoint this young lad I agreed to go up with him. We went up to nearly 140 feet, higher than the hotel, but I have to say it was exciting.

The Band of the 3rd Battalion The Royal Welsh

A flying colleague of mine, Robin Hayes, had a brother who was in the Welsh regimental band. From the early days of Dreamflight Robin managed to persuade the band to come to London and play for the children at the departure party the night before and then to come and march in the hangar the next morning. They continue to do this to this day, and we seem to get more and more members of the band each year. As they march in to the party room at the Renaissance Hotel it is quite spectacular. Can you imagine some forty members of the band led by their mascot Shenkin the goat. The goat has his own special British Airways ID card to enter the hangar! He also has his own little caravan that he sleeps in.

The band have learned quite a few of the Disney theme tunes, etc. and it does seem quite funny hearing them played by a regimental band. Remember, many of these children have probably never have seen a regimental band before.

On the morning of departure they march up and down the hangar with the children marching in between them. Some of them look so proud and the children in wheelchairs are pushed by their escorts. It is a great sight to see the children wearing some of the bands' hats and the band wearing Disney apparel that the children have given them.

When it is time to start boarding the aircraft the children form in to their twelve groups, and one by one each group is "marched" out to the aircraft steps.

The Band have certainly become part of the "Dreamflight" family.

Thank you so much the Band of the Royal Welsh.

20. The Running of Dreamflight

For the first seven years of Dreamflight we had no office support apart from my mother Mollie. As I was still flying it was becoming very difficult to keep up with everything. Bearing in mind that I could be away for up to 21 days on a working trip there was always a big pile of letters when I arrived home, and the answerphone would be full. I would spend all my time off trying to catch up and return peoples' calls. Sometimes I wouldn't get through it all before my next roster. I realised that if you do not get back to people fairly quickly they lose interest and fundraising opportunities could be missed.

Originally the charity was run from home but eventually home was not big enough to store all the equipment and stocks of items that we now needed. We had by now leased a small office in Chartridge in Buckinghamshire and we decided to employ a secretary on a part time basis. We interviewed and decided on Penny Wright in 1992. Penny was invaluable and as time went on we realised we needed to employ her on a full time basis.

When Penny's husband sadly passed away and Penny needed some time off, Jan Wilson, the wife of one of our group leaders offered to come in and answer the phones for us. She worked for us on a part time basis until Fiona Whitehead came and joined us.

In 2005 realising that Penny would be coming up to her retirement we felt that we should employ Penny's replacement to work with her so that Penny could show her the ropes.

After a successful interview Judy Perry was offered the job and is with us to this very day.

In July 2005 we moved offices from Chartridge to Hill Avenue in Amersham on the Hill where we are today. Penny retired in 2005.

In April 2006 Suzanne Harrison came to work for us also on a part time basis replacing Fiona.

In 2009, David Gawn, who had been an escort and a stand-in group leader, came to work for us on a six month contract handling fundraising and communications. I had been retired from BA for five years by this time and I seemed to be busier than ever and it appeared I had given up full time paid employment to have a full time unpaid job! Before David's six month contract was due to expire, David started interviewing candidates for the Fundraising and Communications Manager and in Jan 2010 Emma Rembalski came to work for us.

Emma left us in 2011 and Suzanne left us at the end of March 2012. We now have Caroline on a part time basis and Paula is just about to join us in a full time capacity. The girls in the office have always been so supportive and they have also given up quite a bit of their spare time for the charity as well. Not only that, they have been great fun to work with.

The Trustees

There are currently five trustees who are responsible for all the major decisions of the charity. We are all hands on with everyday decisions as well.

There is myself, Dr. Simon Bailey, Valerie Wright, who used to work on the ground for British Airways, Robert Bass, and David Gawn.

John Tye was a trustee for fifteen years and retired at the end of 2011. Thank you John for all your hard work.

21. How Things have Changed over the Years

Over the years so much has changed, some things for the better and others have brought new challenges.

Technology has changed the course of Dreamflight so much.

Today, with the website, so many of the children that we took back on the first few Dreamflights have got back in touch with us. It is wonderful to hear how they have got on and how they have managed to fight their illness or disability. It is so heartwarming to receive these emails.

We have taken some children back as escorts. One young girl came back as a doctor, another as an escort, and another escort is a Paralympic Gold Medallist, as mentioned in a previous chapter.

The things I don't enjoy so much are the amount of paperwork that we now have to complete because of Health and Safety and Risk Assessment, Moving and Handling, etc., but in this day and age we have to accept it.

Another thing that we have to do every two years is have all the adults that are involved with Dreamflight CRB checked (Criminal Records Board).

We have to have a child protection policy in place, not only for the children but also to protect the adults, and so the paperwork goes on.

But, you know, technology is good. The website is invaluable. We have a Facebook page as well and these are all good instruments for communication, and, it saves on postage!

22. Marriages from Dreamflight Friendships

Over the years so many friendships have been made amongst Dreamflighters and this is very special. Some adults have told me that it not only changes childrens' lives but also the Dreamflight adults. A couple of adults have changed careers after their Dreamflight experience.

Some friendships have developed even further and have resulted in marriages amongst Dreamflighters.

Sheila Scott one of the cabin crew on the very first year married one of the Orlando policemen.

Dr. Simon Bailey met his wife Suzanne as she was a physiotherapist on the trip.

Graeme McAlpine and Melanie were on our video team.

Greig Smith who was a cameraman married an American escort Tina Halliwell

Dave Reilly works for BA as an engineer met his wife Jo Foyle on a Dreamflight trip.

John Swift (cameraman) met and married Laura McGee a nurse.

A cabin crew member when realising she had to fundraise to earn her place on the crew decided to go and enlist the help of her local fire brigade in South Wales. Yes, you have guessed correctly, Carol finished up her fundraising efforts by marrying one of the firemen, Keith Morgan.

23. Wonderful Comments from the Children/Adults and Parents

I thought you might like to read some of the wonderful stories and comments from the children and adults who have been on Dreamflight.

Driving to Discovery Cove in 2010 one of the children had worked out that dolphins live in the sea and that Discovery Cove, where we were going to, was not on the coast. He wanted to know if the dolphins would be arriving by coach!

In 2008 we had one child who was in the Dolphin Group whose birthday was on the day that we were swimming with the dolphins.

I had been told that Discovery Cove did a birthday package for $86 so of course, it had to be done didn't it? At the end of the swim the dolphin nosed up to him with a special buoy with his name and 'Happy Birthday' on it. His group then went to a cabanna at the back of the beach area which had been decorated and once we were all in there they brought in a birthday cake with candles.

I will never forget his face and when the Seaworld lady said to him you must make a wish before you blow the candles out, he said "I don't need to make a wish as all my wishes have already come true this week" Well that was it, all the adults including myself were in tears!

On occasions when I arrive back from the theme parks and am standing by the coffee machine in the hotel lobby watching everyone come in, legs aching and feeling quite tired, all it needs is for one child to come up and put their arms round you and say, "thank you so much I have had the best day of my life"and all the tiredness and everything else just pales in to oblivion.

On one trip a young lad came up and asked me if I would lend him 50 quid. I asked him what he needed it for, "To buy her a present", was his reply. He was referring to the escort who was looking after him.

LETTER FROM A CHILD IN 1998:

Imagine the world you live in is made up of disabled people. Everything revolves around their needs, everything is adjusted for their benefit. There are few healthy people like many of you. The world might have a few advantages, such as no stairs, but here would be many things that you would miss. Imagine how isolated and lonely you would feel, how odd and out of place.

Now imagine for the first time in your life, you get the chance to go away on an amazing holiday with two hundred other people who all had problems, and over 200 volunteers determined to adjust the disabled world so you can have a good time. You finally get to do things you've always wanted, freedom from a restricted world, independence and the chance to meet other people who know how you feel.

It was not the location that made the holiday so special. Anyone, if they have enough money can go to America. It was the knowledge that I was not alone, that there were other people in similar situations that knew what I was going through.

Because I am used to the pain of everyday life, the frequent stays in hospital and the side effects of chemotherapy treatment, they have become normal to me and I tend to dismiss these problems as minor inconveniences. Instead of trying to forget and deny my illness, Dreamflight showed me how to face up to , and be proud of who I am and what I have to offer the world. They showed me that it wasn't abnormal to be "different" but a special quality.

I shall always remember the friends I made – we have a special understanding of each other and a bond that holds us together.

For a week I was pleased to be disabled, because if not, I might never have met these amazing people. We were on a completely different level from the rest of the world. I was with people who understood things that many of you will never understand – how ever hard you try – the pain of disease, the many limitations, the endless struggle to keep going and what it is like to lose your childhood. It definitely was a "Holiday of a Lifetime."

Wonderful Comments From Parents

Here is a selection of comments from some parents over the years.

There is no way that we, as a family, could have given Peter what Dreamflight gave him – the company of other youngsters of his own age, the opportunity to travel away from Mum and Dad, the fun of the early morning swims, and late pizza parties.

When we collected him he had really grown up – his voice had broken, and when we look at the video of the trip we can see the rather nervous children blossom into comedy double acts with cheeky anecdotes and lots of smiles and laughs.

The video enabled the "extended family" too, to share in the fun and jollities, the uncles, aunts, cousins, and grandparents all were heartened by Peter's trip. John and I were so grateful for all that Dreamflight had done that we persuaded them to donate to the charity instead of giving Christmas presents.

FROM ANOTHER PARENT

I have just watched my daughter having the time of her life in Florida with Dreamflight. The video is breathtaking and I cannot put into words how fantastic it has been seeing her and the rest of the children, and adults alike, having such a great time.

You gave my daughter the opportunity to experience a magical ten days which she would not have missed for the world. I asked her which bit of Dreamflight she enjoyed the most. Every time I ask, she gives me the same answer every time "ALL OF IT".

This poem was written by a parent of a child on the first Dreamflight in 1987. She handed it to me with a basket of flowers on our return.

288 children on a Jumbo Jet
On a flight I don't think they will forget
Up up up and away
Bound for Disneyworld in the USA
The children handicapped or disabled they may be
But the expression on their faces was a joy to see
Money was raised with this flight in view
By different people and British Airways too
VIP treatment by royalty and stars galore
Was a little bit extra that was in store
And for making this Dreamflight come true
As the parents of one of the children
Can I just say THANK YOU

Wonderful Comments From Escorts
A MESSAGE FROM ONE OF OUR PHYSIOTHERAPISTS:

How can I sum up my first year on Dreamflight? Exhilarating, emotional, humbling, hilarious, fun, and oh yes, utterly exhausting! Dreamflight has really meant the world to me and it is an amazing charity which brings so much happiness and fun into the lives of the children we take. It is one of the most enriching things that I have ever done. And, for those people who were jealous of me going on a "holiday" before I went, believe me it wasn't! It was more than just a holiday, it was a trip of lifetime for everyone on the trip, children and adults alike.

FROM ONE OF OUR DOCTORS. (2010)

The bottom line for me, was that last year was quite possibly the best trip that I have been on, it was a huge success. One of the boys that I looked after was deaf and also on permanent intravenous feed, which has made going on holiday and anytime away from his mum impossible. On arriving back he said he does not care if he cannot go away again because he will always have the Dreamflight memories. Reminds you of just how amazing Dreamflight is and what a fantastic experience that it has made possible. Thank you Dr James Hayden.

FROM ONE OF THE TRAINERS AT DISCOVERY COVE

"My name is Katy and I have been a dolphin trainer at Discovery Cove for five years. I just wanted to write and let you know that the Dreamflight programme is just amazing. We, as trainers, look forward to Dreamflight

144

every year, and many trainers want to come in on their days off to be part of this special day.

This year I was at Magic Kingdom with my family and we saw all the kids and chaperones walking and laughing and having a grand time. I explained to my parents who Dreamflight was and they were so impressed with how everyone was so happy and well behaved in the parks. It was cool and made me even more excited for their day at Discovery Cove later in the week.

Well, that's it. Dreamflight is awesome and Discovery Cove Trainers look forward to seeing you every year

A LETTER FROM A GUEST IN ONE OF THE THEME PARKS

I just thought I would drop you a quick line. I have just returned from holiday in Florida with my family, including 20 month old twins. We had the pleasure of bumping into some of your Dreamflight kids during an outing to Seaworld. Each group had a specific theme, and everyone was dressed to impress. My children thought they looked fantastic in their hats, wigs and co-ordinating T shirts. I can safely say, I don't think I've ever seen such a bunch of delighted, happy, or excited people on holiday. I hope they all had a great time, your helpers were all great. Good luck with your work.

LETTER FROM A CHILD NOW GROWN UP

20 years ago I was a nervous, excited, tired (due to lack of sleep the previous night!) 11 year old little girl, sitting in the hotel at Heathrow Airport about to embark on my first ever holiday abroad.

I can remember the day like it was yesterday. I was

145

meeting and greeting many famous faces. That holiday was a memory that I still carry with me today.

I am now a happily married mother with three beautiful children.

Disney in Florida is the family's favourite place to go when we are choosing our annual holiday. I have been fortunate enough to return to this magical place a further four times. In 2005 I took my husband and children, my baby being just eight weeks old, for the first time. Even my husband fell in love with the place.

So on your 20th Anniversary I wanted to send my heart filled thanks and wish you all the best for the future.

Thanks again for making my dreams come true 20 years ago. Always in my heart and memories.

FROM THE PARENTS OF A CHILD IN 2010

My son left for Florida as my little boy, but that boy never returned! Instead I got a young man who is far more comfortable about who he is, what he thinks, what he needs from me (and what he now no longer needs from me).

Brings tears to your eyes doesn't it?

24. Awards and Special Events

I have listed here some of the wonderful awards that I have been honoured with over the years, and some special events I have been invited to attend.

The very first award we were given was the Celebrities Guild of Great Britain award in 1989. We had been nominated by Shirley Bowers and Loretta McCullough who worked in the cabin crew scheduling department of British Airways.

We were invited to the Royal Garden Hotel in London and it was a very special dinner followed by the Award ceremony.

A number of years later I was given a further award from the Guild.

Buckingham Palace Garden Party

On 18th July 1995 we were invited to a garden party at Buckingham Palace. It is quite an incredible feeling when you drive through the gates of the palace. You are then escorted through some of the ground floor rooms of the palace and into the gardens. They are beautiful to say the least. There are big marquees erected where you can collect your tea and sandwiches and scones. The Queen arrives and mingles with guests for a while. All too soon, it is over.

You know, you never set out on a project expecting any rewards, so you can imagine how I felt when this letter arrived from the Lord Chamberlain's Office asking if I minded being nominated for an MBE. It was not to say you had got it, but my name was being put forward and I would not know until June when it would be announced in The Daily Telegraph and The Times. They asked you not to tell anyone

about it. Can you imagine having to keep it secret, but on the other hand, you didn't want to go round telling everyone just in case you weren't given the award!

I was up in Scotland on a golfing holiday with twenty of my 747 friends. I received a telephone message at the hotel to call a newspaper. When I rang they said, "you are obviously aware of what you are going to be given tomorrow." So that was how I came to realise that I had been awarded an MBE from the Queen.

I went back to the dinner table and my friends kept saying "Is everything alright, is your Mum OK?" When I shared the news with them I can tell you it cost me quite a bit of money in champagne that night! I flew home the next day, one day ahead of the rest of the group. They managed to get a message to the captain of the flight from Aberdeen back to London and he announced it on the aircraft.

I arrived home and my neighbours had already found out and John, Karen, Tom, Heather, and Jack McNeill had hung a sheet on the garage door. Can you imagine my surprise as I drove down the drive.

It did make me laugh though, I am so grateful to have such wonderful neighbours.

In the November my brother and sister in law (Derek and Beth) flew up from Sydney to be with me on my big day. It was 13th November 1997 an I was going to drive them and my mum in to London, but was told by a friend, Gillian Conway, "No way, her partner, Chris Woods would drive me". Well, can you imagine, at just after 8 a.m. Chris backed down my drive in this big dark blue Bentley, so I arrived in London in style.

When I arrived home that evening, my neighbour John was asking where I had been during the day. I said to him "You know where I have

been." He replied "I had given your car registration number to a couple of his police motor bike colleagues and they were going to escort me in to London, but because I hadn't used my own car they had missed me.

It was an awesome experience. I had spent two months flying with the Queen in my flying days but this was something really special.

Although it does not change you as a person, it sometimes opens doors for the charity. It gives some credibility to the organisation.

Award of Excellence from British Airways

In March 1988 we were given an award for excellence presented by Sir Colin Marshall (as he was then) in recognition of our charitable "Dreamflight" efforts.

In May 1988 I was put through to another tier of the awards and was successful in being selected. We were taken to Vienna for the weekend. I saw the Lippizannier horses, went to hear a wonderful recital, and for a fantastic dinner in one of the palaces.

No 1 Downing Street for Tea

In October 1996 I was taken aback when we were invited to take a group of children for afternoon tea with the then Prime Minister John Major. What an absolutely charming man and not at all like the "grey man" that the press so often made him out to be. John Major seems so different when you actually meet him in person, he is very charismatic.

We all met up at a Heathrow Hotel and went into London on a British Airways coach. Just the children and some of the escorts. Again parents were "banned"!

We decided we would go into London early in case we hit any traffic problems, and if not, we would drive around London for awhile and show the children some of the sights. Whilst we were driving around, one of the children asked me why we weren't going straight there. I said, "Oh well, Norma Major hasn't quite finished making the sandwiches

above: My mum on the left. I am so pleased she managed to do some of the wonderful things with me.

150

for us yet". You know how it is when chatting with children and we started discussing our favourite sandwiches. I was telling them that when I was little my parents didn't have a lot of money and I used to like tomato ketchup sandwiches. Can you imagine my horror about two hours later being presented with tomato ketchup sandwiches in No. 10. Apparently the children had told the waitress that these were my favourite. They had to go up to John and Norma Majors' private kitchen to get the ketchup.

I was talking with John Major (who had just come back from Prime Ministers' question time at the Houses of Parliament) and said what a change this must be for him from dealing with affairs of state and then having to deal with these children. His reply "probably about the same Pat".

Childrens' Christmas Carol Concert

British Airways were holding a childrens' Christmas carol concert at Guildford Cathedral. Several of the BA supported charities were invited to do a reading, and I was one of those selected.

I am not normally thrown by public speaking but to have to do a reading from the Bible is something different. The cathedral was packed and they had two big screens on either side of the cathedral so that everyone could see you. I was sat in the first row pew with Lord Marshall and his wife. I have to admit that the reading made me quite nervous. If you make a mistake when you are just speaking about the charity, it is not the same as making a mistake reading a passage in the Bible. I do not rehearse for my normal speeches but I certainly did for this one!

The London Eye and the Dome

In the year 2000 we accepted a very kind offer from British Airways for 24 past Dreamflight children to visit two of the hottest attractions in London. Namely the London Eye and The Dome. This happened on the 7th and 8th May 2000.

Twenty four children (two from each group) were chosen from the 1999 trip. We checked everyone into the Excelsior Hotel near Heathrow

Airport for the weekend. On the Saturday we went to the London Eye. It was a wonderfully clear day and we could see for miles. We were all surprised how slow and smooth the wheel turned. There were 40 of us altogether and therefore split into two groups of 20 in each capsule. As usual we managed to "jump" the queue. I think it is a Dreamflight technique!

When we checked in to the hotel one of the receptionists asked one of the children when she was going to Florida. Her reply was "in October", the poor receptionist thought we were staying in the hotel until then. Bearing in mind this was May!

During the evening the BA Transport Department were kind enough to lend us a crew bus and a driver and we went off to Spaggio's an Italian restaurant in Slough. Here the management were kind enough to offer two dinners for the price of one!

On Monday we boarded a bus for our journey to "The Dome." On our journey into London one little girl decided that she was desperate for the toilet. Not having one on the bus the driver very kindly parked on a double yellow line in Knightsbridge and she hopped of the bus straight in to McDonalds to use their facilities.

The "Body Zone" in The Dome was a great favourite with most of the children. The acrobat show was fantastic and very colourful. On another computer based attraction you were given a million pounds to spend in one minute. One of the boys managed to spend all but £50.00. His comment "I wish it was real money"!

I didn't manage to go to the "Timelapse" but I was told it was a nightmare for the adults. I never did mange to find out why.

Dinner with Sir Cliff and Tony Blair

Sir Cliff organised a dinner for 40 people at Hampton Court Palace down by the river.

Gloria Hunniford, Cilla Black, and several other celebrity friends of Sir Cliff were invited together with Tony and Cherie Blair.

I had been at a meeting at Heathrow in the afternoon and had changed at one of the local hotels and set out from Heathrow at 5.30 p.m. to get to Hampton Court by 7.00 p.m. This journey normally takes about 25 minutes. What I had not factored in to my schedule was the fact that the Hampton Court Flower Show was on that day. At 7 p.m. I was nowhere near the end of my journey. I was stuck in traffic that was moving about 1 inch every twenty minutes. I rang my friend Robin Williams who is a dear friend of Sir Cliff and explained my predicament. I phoned Robin again at 7.30 p.m. and he said not to worry as Tony and Cherie were also stuck in traffic. I eventually arrived at 7.50 p.m.(nearly two and a half hours for a journey that normally takes 25 mins). I was rushed into the palace and everyone had just gone into dinner, but as Sir Cliff knew that I was literally seconds away he kept everyone standing until I walked in the room. So nice of him. I would have felt so embarrassed walking in once everyone had been seated.

Dorton House School for the Blind

I had the great privelege to be invited to Dorton House School for the Blind in Sevenoaks on 25th July 1997 to present their prizes at the end of the school year.

I would like to explain that my Aunt had been a teacher at this school and I had visited the school on many occasions since I was about fourteen years old. The one thing that fascinated me was when you walk into a class of sighted children they all look up. You walk into a class of blind children and they all put their heads down and listen. They then like to stroke you to feel what you are wearing. At the age of fourteen I would never ever have imagined that I would be so honoured as to be invited back to present the prizes.

I would also like to mention that my aunt had lived in Guernsey and had been a teacher there and in memory of her I wanted to invite a child from Guernsey on Dreamflight. Gerry Girard, who was a pilot of BA and whom I had known since I was a child, organised a big fundraising evening at Old Government House in St. Peter Port. I flew over for the event which was going to be televised by Channel TV. We had already selected a child from the island and she, together with her parents, arrived for the evening. She was introduced to me and I said to her "I am going on TV very shortly talking about my life as a stewardess, would you like to come and sit on the sofa with me so that your friends will be able to see you". Of course, she agreed. Once the cameras were rolling I explained to her that there was something else I did apart from being a stewardess. I explained about Dreamflight and then invited her to come on the trip that year. Well, she was dumbfounded, everyone including the TV crew were in tears.

25. One Dream Away –
The Dreamflight Song

In 1990 Rory Macdonald (who was, at that time, the Donald Duck Group Leader) and a purser with British Airways for his "day job" met Barry Mason at lunch with a friend. Rory got chatting with Barry and was soon telling him all about Dreamflight – little knowing that Barry Mason was one of the most prolific songwriters of the 60s and 70s with Delilah being one of his biggest hits.

The result of all this was Barry wrote a song and donated it to Dreamflight called "One Dream Away". This is always played on the childrens' videos that they receive after their trip.

I only wish I could play this for you, but being just a book it is not possible.

One Dream Away

Where is tomorrow
Nobody knows
But when you're dreaming
Anything goes
Whatever you're seeking
You'll find it some day
Just close your eyes
It's one dream away
My arms around you
Your hand holding mine

Let's drift off together
Anywhere will be fine
You'll never be lonely
'Cos I'm going to stay
Right here beside you
One Dream Away
Take a ride on a rainbow
Hold on tight
Take a little ride on a rainbow
It's going to be alright
This is your Dreamflight
Now and forever
This feeling will last
And lie on in our hearts
When this moment has passed
Now you know I love you
So believe what I say
They're waiting for you ...
... And they do really come true
Dream Away
It's your dream today.

26. The 25th Anniversary

The 25th year of Dreamflight was very special for me. I could never have dreamed back in 1986 that the charity would still be going after 25 years. As I have said before, it was supposed to be a "one off" trip.

A very dedicated team of Dreamflighters formed a committee to set about organising a special anniversary day.

This was set for Saturday 27th August 2011 and was held at the British Airways Concorde Club near Heathrow Airport. It was to take the form of a family fun day with BBQ and the evening would be a black tie dinner.

It was an amazing day. All of the groups had a stall set up and they had so many photographs and pieces of memorabilia from over the years.

The RAF flew in a Merlin helicopter, the lads have been fundraising for Dreamflight for many years. We had the Queen's Special Escort motorcycle team there with their motorbikes. The police dogs and their handlers were also there.

The BA simulator was a great hit with everyone. It was a challenge for people to "try and fly an aeroplane like the real pilots!", and the BA bouncy castle for the younger children to play on. The BA brass band were on hand to play music and played "The Battle of Britain" as the Merlin helicopter flew in.

I was talking to the committee just a few days before the event and they were thrilled that about 800 people were planning on attending the event.

On the day just over 1100 people turned up. What a fantastic surprise. More burgers and hot dogs were needed.

It was fantastic for me to be able to chat to so many "Dreamflighters" be they past children from the flights or the escorts from over the years.

Several children from the original flight in 1987 had come along including Nyree Lewis (now Kindred) who won a medal at the Beijing Paralympic Games. So wonderful to see Nyree with her new baby.

Another couple of girls came and told me that they had been on Dreamflight 20 years ago, and had been room mates. They said that, as they lived in different parts of the country, they still manage to meet up for a week every year. Fantastic that they have become life long friends.

There were so many wonderful stories that day that I cannot possibly list them all. People came from all over the country for the event and it was brilliant watching them all chatting and catching up with events in their lives.

The day was finished off with a black tie dinner, and the surprise at the very end came when they announced that although this was not supposed to be a fundraising event, an amount of £40,000 had been raised. I could not believe it. I am so grateful for everyone that participated in this event and made it such a wonderful celebration for Dreamflight. Even the weather was kind to us and the sun shone for most of the day - just one quick shower and that was it.

above: Pat with the 25th Anniversary Committee.

27. The Continuing Story . . .

After my cancer in 2004 (the only year I couldn't go on the trip) it has made me more determined than ever that more children will have their "Holiday of a Lifetime" and hopefully a life changing experience. I have got to this age without having to have such invasive treatment, but these children are having it at such a young age. They do definitely deserve a treat in life. Having "sampled" some of the treatment if I can help motivate, inspire, give hope and courage to these children then my illness will not have been in vain.

'A dream you dream alone is only a dream. A dream you dream together is a reality.' – Mr John Lennon.

I entirely agree with this. Thank you everyone for making my dream come true and making Dreamflight a reality.

Throughout my life I have been extremely fortunate. The things I have done, and the people I have met, either through my flying career or through Dreamflight, have been wonderful and I can't thank you enough for just being a friend. I have always believed

*"Life should NOT be a journey to the grave with
the intention of arriving safely in an attractive and
well preserved body, but rather to skid in sideways –
Chardonnay in one hand – chocolate in the other – body
thoroughly used up and screaming WOW!
(By Hunter S Thompson)*

I have now been chosen as an Olympic Torch Bearer on the 9th July and so the story goes on ...

A proportion of the profit from sales of this book is being donated to Dreamflight.